TABLE OF CONTENTS

INTRODUCING THE COLLECTOR'S VALUE GUIDE™

*W*elcome! Whether you're a longtime fan of the Collector's Value Guide™ or are just becoming familiar with our collectible titles, you're sure to be thrilled with this, our third edition of the Collector's Value Guide to Department 56 Villages. We've put this guide together in an easy-to-use format and filled it with tons of great information that is sure to add to your enjoyment of the holiday tradition that has become a year-round sensation.

Heritage Village & Snow Village

Because each Department 56 village has its own unique character, we're delighted to offer separate, comprehensive overviews for each, as well as a look at the history of Department 56. Also included is the latest news in releases and retirements, as well as a showcase of the top ten most valuable buildings for each village. Next comes the expanded Value Guide section with large, full-color pictures of every building and accessory, as well as variations. Every retired piece features up-to-date 1998 secondary market values and there's room at the bottom of each page to total the value of your collection.

Plus More!

In addition to the accurate, timely information of the Value Guide, we've included more sections to educate and entertain. You can take our trivia quizzes for both Heritage Village and Snow Village, find out how to maneuver on the secondary market, improve your display prowess with our expanded display section, discover the history behind the pieces in the *Historical Landmark Series* and much, much more. Enjoy the journey!

*S*ince their debut in 1976, Department 56 lighted houses have captured the imagination of collectors everywhere. Each year at holiday time, buildings from The Heritage Village Collection and The Original Snow Village are unpacked, dusted off and set up in homes all across the country. But if you've been bitten by the Department 56 bug, you know that it's much more than a holiday tradition. It's grown to a year-round craze that has transformed the collectibles landscape!

Department 56 began as part of a large flower and garden store in Minnesota called Bachman's; the store's "Department 56" was where the wholesale gift imports division was located. Ed Bazinet, the founder of Department 56 as we know it, was in charge of this department when he took a fateful Christmas journey to a quaint little town along Minnesota's St. Croix River. The town was bedecked in holiday splendor, complete with garlands festooning lampposts and carolers singing Christmas songs. This picture-postcard scene evoked many fine memories for Bazinet, and he decided to recapture some of those feelings for others. Bazinet developed the first six lighted buildings and, in 1976, introduced "Snow Village."

Since its inception, Snow Village has depicted small town American life from the 1930s to today, with the buildings and accessories conjuring up a sense of nostalgia that collectors love. The line was a success, and in 1979, in an effort to keep the collection a manageable size, the first ten retirements were announced.

In order to avoid confusion with the growing number of imitators, the village underwent a name change and became "The Original Snow Village" in 1983. In 1984, Department 56 released a line of buildings inspired by Charles Dickens' writings about Victorian London. *Dickens' Village* was an immediate hit!

In 1986, two more villages, *New England Village* and *Alpine Village,* were introduced under the heading of "Heritage Village." These were followed in 1987 by *Christmas in the City* and *Little Town of Bethlehem*, the only village to be released as a complete set. Department 56 announced the first retirements for *Dickens' Village* in 1989, and introduced *North Pole* two years later. The *Disney Parks Village Series* was issued in 1994.

In 1992, Bachman's sold Department 56 to Forstmann, Little & Co., a New York-based investment firm. Bazinet stayed on as CEO, and the company began to offer stock to the public through the New York Stock Exchange. While many held their collective breath, there turned out to be no reason for concern. Forstmann, Little & Co. has not only maintained the high standards of its predecessor, but has expanded the product line as well. Susan Engel took over as CEO in 1996.

Department 56 opens their Minnesota showroom Friday afternoons in the summer months. For more information, please write or call:

Department 56
One Village Place Showroom Tour
6436 City West Parkway
Eden Prairie, MN 55344
1-800-LIT-TOWN

In addition to all the great pieces that have been released, some of the other highlights of recent years include the May 1996 retirement of the entire *Disney Parks Village Series*. In 1997, the company began separating sets so that pieces could be bought individually.

The Original Snow Village and the seven villages that make up Heritage Village offer collectors a wide variety of buildings and accessories from which to choose pieces for the perfect holiday (or year-round) display. Whole families can get involved in designing and displaying vignettes from yesteryear, sharing in the joys of being together and taking delight in the collection.

Under Construction

Snow Village and Heritage Village buildings are constructed in much the same way. After researching the era and style of a proposed building, drawings are made and are then used as blueprints. Each building is sculpted from clay and has an imprinted bottomstamp which features the name of the piece, the logo for the village, the issue year and the Department 56 copyright symbol.

To create a building, molds are made, and liquid clay, also known as slip, is poured into them. After the slip hardens, the buildings are removed, and gently sanded. Windows are cut and attachments are "glued" into place with slip. Finally, the buildings are ready for a series of firings in special ovens, called kilns. After eight hours in the kilns, which heat to temperatures of over 1000 degrees, the buildings are slowly cooled. The pieces are then handpainted. Buildings from Snow Village go back into the kiln, this time to harden the clear overglaze. Buildings for Heritage Village have a matte finish, and antiquing paints are often used to give certain pieces a weathered look. No glaze is used, but the buildings do have to take another trip to the kiln, at lower temperatures and for a shorter period of time, to set the colors.

The Heritage Village Collection consists of seven individual villages, each one with its own distinctive flavor. Whether you like the hustle and bustle of city life or the serenity of a New England pastoral scene, there is sure to be a village for you!

Dickens' Village

*S*tarted in 1984, *Dickens' Village* quickly became a collectors' favorite. Inspired by the writings of English author Charles Dickens, the village transports you back to the days of Victorian London.

Take a trip with the ghost of Christmas past! The streets of London look grand with the freshly fallen snow and holiday decorations. Walk by "Gad's Hill Place," and stop for a few minutes to listen to Mr. Dickens himself, as he reads "A Christmas Carol" to a rapt crowd. Before you travel on, warm up with some freshly made gingerbread and a cup of hot apple cider from a vendor.

See the sights as you catch a ride on the "Red Christmas Sulky" and trot past the "Tower of London," "Victoria Station" and "Ramsford Palace." Don't forget to stop by Portobello Road where costermongers, also known as peddlers, hawk their fruits and vegetables, and shop windows beckon. Finally, quench your thirst with a big draught of stout and a kidney pie at the pub, before you are awakened from your reverie and realize that you are back home once again! Was it all a dream?

Even if it was, you can still recreate the fantasy with the 113 lighted buildings in *Dickens' Village*. Although many have been retired, 28 buildings are currently available. Many accessories complement the village, and are just waiting to transform your bay window, dining room hutch or fireplace mantel into a scene straight out of one of Dickens' novels. The styles cover all facets of Victorian English life, from the countryside farmhouses and small shops to the stately manors of the blue bloods and aristocrats.

If you're a Charles Dickens fan, you will enjoy the many reflections of his work found in the village. Dickens' canon serves as a rich source for the buildings and accessories. Straight from *A Christmas Carol* come renditions of "Scrooge & Marley's Counting House" and "The Cottage Of Bob Cratchit & Tiny Tim." "Betsy Trotwood's Cottage" and "Mr. Wickfield Solicitor" make you want to read *David Copperfield* again!

But you don't have to be a book lover to appreciate *Dickens' Village*. History buffs will admire the accuracy and detail of "The Old Curiosity Shop," a rendition of an actual shop built in 1567. The "Sir John Falstaff Inn," a pub named for one of Shakespeare's characters, and "Gad's Hill Place," the home of Charles Dickens, are now considered historical landmarks and have been recreated as *Dickens' Village* buildings. The 1998 release for the *Historical Landmark Series* is "The Old Globe Theatre," a replica of the building where Shakespeare first presented his plays so long ago. The building is Department 56's interpretation of how the theater may have looked if it had still been standing in Dickens' day. What a wonderful blend of history and imagination!

New England Village

*M*aybe your vision of Christmas in New England involves a bustling seaport where you can taste the salt in the air and the beacon from the lighthouse blinks steadily. Perhaps it's a pastoral landscape, with a new layer of snow, or a quaint little village dressed in holiday finery, with the requisite church and carolers on the town green. *New England Village* has all of these and more to indulge your holiday fantasies!

New England Village was introduced in 1986 with seven lit buildings. It has since grown to include 51 buildings, 14 of which are currently available. Many of the buildings bear the names of actual landmarks, such as the "Old North Church," where lit lamps signalled to the colonists that the British were coming. Others are flights of fancy, like the "Sleepy Hollow" set. New for this year are "East Willet Pottery," "Semple's Smokehouse" and "Steen's Maple House."

These buildings reflect the "Yankee" mentality: they have clean lines, simple yet stable architecture and are made with more than a pinch of good common sense! The accessories include covered bridges, a maple sugaring shed and hard-working lobster trappers; three common fixtures of any genuine New England village!

Alpine Village

D epartment 56 crossed the ocean for inspiration to create *Alpine Village*, set in the German, Swiss or Austrian Alps. If you listen carefully, you might hear the strains of far-off violins playing a waltz, or red-faced children calling "Aufwiedersehen," as they hurry home to where cups of hot "schokolade" and honey cakes await them. Sounds like a scene right out of *Heidi*, doesn't it?

As a matter of fact, "Heidi & Her Goats" do live here now, as a new release for the 1998 line of accessories. In addition to Heidi and her friends, *Alpine Village* also features a new toy store called "Spielzeug Laden." Originally introduced as a set of five buildings in 1986, *Alpine Village* has expanded to 18 lighted buildings, with 8 currently available.

The pointed roofs and colorful facades of the buildings are a stark contrast to the snow-laden ground which climbs up around them. As with the other villages, *Alpine Village* has a bit of history to it, as well. "St. Nikolaus Kirche" is based on the church where "Silent Night" was first heard, and there's even a music box in the village that plays that song. A set of accessories entitled "Climb Every Mountain" recalls the bravery of the Von Trapp family as they made their escape from the German-occupied countryside.

Christmas in the City

*S*ome people thrive on the excitement of city life, and Department 56 has infused *Christmas in the City* with that spirit. You don't even have to step outside your door to bring the wonderful sights and sounds of the big city right into your home.

Carolers sing outside the door of "Hollydale's Department Store." On your way out, put a few crisp bills into Santa's kettle for those less fortunate. After all, 'tis the season! You can go uptown to the art museum and see a fabulous impressionist exhibit, and afterwards head on over to Chinatown where you can meet up with friends at that fabulous restaurant everyone's been talking about. The festivities continue at the "Hi-De-Ho Nightclub" where you can dance until the wee hours of the morning. Whew! That's exhausting! But you don't have to worry about the long ride ahead, because you never even left your living room!

Introduced in 1987 with just six buildings, construction in the city has just not quit! The booming metropolis now includes 43 buildings, 14 of which are currently available. This year's introductions include "Johnson's Grocery & Deli," "Riverside Row Shops" and "The Capitol," an impressive structure destined to become the centerpiece for many collectors' *Christmas in the City* displays. *Christmas in the City* throbs with the pulse of city life: the culture, the commerce, the people.

North Pole

*W*ell, here it is at last – proof that Santa really does exist. Don't you believe in Santa? Well, if you didn't before, you will after visiting the *North Pole*! Gumdrop-laden trees hang over walkways lined with candy canes and the whole village is abuzz with excitement. After all, there are only 131 days until Christmas, and the clock is ticking!

One of Santa's elves will be happy to give you a tour. Walk over to "Santa's Lookout Tower" and survey the scene below. You can see Comet and Vixen and all the rest of the reindeer munching fresh hay, and hear the approaching supply train's whistle though it's still a few miles away.

The sounds of machines whirring and hammers banging greet you as you enter the "Elfin Forge & Assembly Shop," where cars and trucks are made. Over at the "North Pole Dolls & Santa's Bear Works," elves are working on Raggedy Ann™ dolls and stuffed bunnies. Everything you see has been touched by the joy and happiness that is Christmas!

Three buildings started the *North Pole* in 1991. "Santa's Workshop," the "Elf Bunkhouse," and "Reindeer Barn" were erected not a moment too soon, because Santa had work to do! The village now has 36 buildings, with 18 currently available. There are four new buildings for this year, including "Glass Ornament Works," "Mrs. Claus' Greenhouse," "Santa's Light Shop" and a new limited edition piece, "Elsie's Gingerbread."

Disney Parks Village Series

E very year millions of people flock to the Disney
parks in California and Florida,
and look for mementos to take home.
Department 56 started the *Disney Parks
Village Series* with these folks in mind.
The buildings, based on those found in
the popular tourist attractions, were
made available to the public three
months after their initial release to the
Disney parks.

Consisting of six lighted buildings and four accessories, the *Disney Parks Village Series* sought to cap-
ture a bit of the Disney magic. However, the company surprised collectors by announcing the retirement
of the entire village in May of 1996. The last two
pieces, "Silversmith" and "Tinker Bell's Treasures"
were available for only a short period of time
before their retirement.

Little Town Of Bethlehem

L ittle Town Of Bethlehem was introduced in 1987
as a complete twelve-piece set depicting the
birth of Jesus. There are three lighted buildings in this
nativity scene. Other pieces include Mary, Joseph and
the baby Jesus, as well as the Three Wise Men, a camel
and an array of other animals and trees. This set is currently available.

*T*here are 18 new releases for Heritage Village buildings (including two sets) and a total of 26 new accessories. Of the building releases, six are for *Dickens' Village* (plus one Canadian exclusive), three for *New England Village*, one for *Alpine Village*, three for *Christmas in the City* and four for *North Pole*.

Dickens' Village

Ashwick Lane Hose & Ladder . . . With so many thatched roofs in town, it was only a matter of time before the first firehouse was built in *Dickens' Village!* With its crimson color, sloping roof and sharp angles, "Ashwick Lane Hose & Ladder" is one of the most striking of the 1998 releases. The tall side tower houses the alarm bell, while the widow's walk gives the firefighters a clear view of the village – the best vantage point from which to look for smoke or listen for shouts of "Fire, ho!" from the streets.

Crooked Fence Cottage . . . The wooden fence that circles this aptly-named abode isn't the only thing that's crooked! There are jagged steps winding around to the back and the multi-sectioned thatch roof seems to bulge unevenly. The huge brick chimney, riven by gaping cracks, looks like it's seen better days! Collectors looking to add a little character to their village displays need look no further than "Crooked Fence Cottage!"

East Indies Trading Co. . . . Reflecting the long history of British overseas commercial ventures, the "East Indies Trading Co." will make a fantastic addition to your village's commercial life. Inside the stately brick and wood warehouse, villagers will find a dazzling array of merchandise from exotic and faraway lands. A special recolored version of this piece called the "Canadian Trading Co." will be available from Department 56 retailers in Canada.

Leacock Poulterer . . . The townspeople of *Dickens' Village* haven't enjoyed the services of a poultry shop since the 1993 retirement of the "Poulterer" from the "Merchant Shops" (set/5). Part of the *Christmas Carol Revisited* series, "Leacock Poulterer" opens its doors in 1998. Among the great design elements are a thick wooden fence, front shutters which open, and a trio of geese displayed in the window.

Manchester Square (set/25) . . . With "Manchester Square," Department 56 has introduced the largest *Dickens' Village* set ever! It consists of four unique shops: "Custom House," "Frogmore Chemist," "G. Choir's Weights & Scales" and "Lydby Trunk & Satchel Shop." The set also comes with display accessories, including trees, a cobblestone road and snow.

The Old Globe Theatre (set/4, LE-1998) . . . The second release in the *Historical Landmark Series*, "The Old Globe Theatre" is available only through the end of 1998. Based on Shakespeare's Globe Theatre, its design reflects a vision of what the building may have looked like had it survived to Dickens' day (turn to page 190 for the history of the actual Globe Theatre). Notably, the interior of the building is visible through the roof. If you add only one piece this year, be sure to make it "The Old Globe Theatre!"

Dickens' Village Accessories . . . Eight new accessories have been introduced for 1998. "Ashley Pond Skating Party" (set/6) depicts a group of villagers having fun on the ice, and a merchant tempts passersby with her holiday sweets in "Christmas Pudding Costermonger" (set/3). The mystery of Christmas is revealed in "Father Christmas's Journey," while "The Fire Brigade Of London Town" (set/5) depicts a battalion of fire-fighters rushing to extinguish a blaze. "Nine Ladies Dancing" (set/2) and "Ten Pipers Piping" (set/3) are new releases in *The Twelve Days of Dickens' Village* series, and "Dickens' Village Church" and "Old Curiosity Shop" are contribu-tions to the *Classic Ornament Series.*

New England Village

East Willet Pottery . . . Taking its title from a common New England surname, "East Willet Pottery" brings another talented artisan to the growing community. The building's brick foundation, brown shingled roof and tall brick chimney convey a sense of earthy cre-ation. The main portion of the building is where the potter sells his wares, but the real magic takes place in the attached firing house and kiln.

Semple's Smokehouse . . . What *New England Village* display would be complete without the town smokehouse? Once the workday begins, the scent of hickory smoked beef and pork entices villagers from all around. The build-ing's design makes it a perfect fit just at the edge of a forest or up on a hill: its stone foundation, towering chimney and uneven, roughly-tiled roof give it a "hard-working" look.

Steen's Maple House . . . Few things are as distinctly "New England" as maple sugaring and this tradition is honored with the release of "Steen's Maple House." The thick, sweet scent of maple hangs in the air around the shed, and is reflected in the real "smoking" feature of the piece. Whether your villagers prefer the syrup or the candy, "Steen's Maple House" is sure to satisfy everyone with a sweet tooth!

New England Village Accessories . . . Among the new accessories for 1998 are three additions to the growing Christmas Bazaar. "Christmas Bazaar . . . Flapjacks & Hot Cider" (set/2) depicts a matronly merchant selling hot food and drink. Of course, the marketplace wouldn't be complete without "Christmas Bazaar . . . Toy Vendor & Cart" (set/2), and for collectors who display these themed accessories together, there is the "Christmas Bazaar . . . Sign" (set/2). Also new this year is "Tapping The Maples" (set/7), which brings the new sugaring shed to life with a bustling sap-gathering scene, and for the *Classic Ornament Series*, there's the new "Craggy Cove Lighthouse."

Alpine Village

Spielzeug Laden . . . Everything about this new toy shop says "fun," from the smiley-face clock, to the jester on the tower, to the paper doll silhouettes that line the upper balcony. The green roof, red trim and blue shut-

ters of "Spielzeug Laden" make it impossible to miss against the snowy hills. That can only mean lots of attention from the *Alpine Village* kid community!

Alpine Village Accessories . . . The newest accessory for the village is "Heidi & Her Goats" (set/4). The friendly goats appear to be causing a little trouble for a passing gentleman!

Christmas in the City

The Capitol . . . This grand seat of state government sports a center dome perched atop a circle of golden pillars and flanked by pairs of smaller domes on both sides. Two golden lions grace the rooftop, while a long set of steps leads lawmakers and private citizens to the front doors. Sharp-eyed collectors may want to compare the actual piece with the picture provided here, for "The Capitol" will feature additional color highlights by the time it reaches retailers' shelves.

Johnson's Grocery & Deli . . . "Johnson's Grocery & Deli" will be a popular stop for city shoppers, who haven't had a new grocery store since "Hank's Market" retired in 1992. Reminiscent of shops found in New York's Soho district, this bright building sports alternating reds and yellows, making it easy to spot from down the street. A flower stand and a fine assortment of fruits and vegetables also brighten up the city sidewalk.

Riverside Row Shops . . . Reflecting the "shoulder to shoulder" look common among city buildings, the "Riverside Row Shops" will let city dwellers knock off a few errands, whether they need to stop at the "National Bank," the "Riverside Barber Shop" (the first ever in the collection), or "Crosby & Smith Stationers."

Christmas in the City Accessories . . . There are four new accessories and two new ornaments in the collection this year. In "Big Smile For The Camera" (set/2), a starlet gets together with young fans for a snapshot while a photographer waits patiently. "Johnson's Grocery . . . Holiday Deliveries" comes in very handy during the busy holiday season, while the three women and three children in "Let's Go Shopping In The City" (set/3) find shopping too tempting to pass up. Finally, there is the elegant "Spirit Of The Season," a sculpture of a golden angel mounted atop a fountain. Two new ornaments in the *Classic Ornament Series* are "Dorothy's Dress Shop" and "City Hall."

North Pole

Elsie's Gingerbread (LE-1998) . . . There's no mistaking this limited edition's gingerbread house look, or the sweet scent of molasses and brown sugar that mean a fresh batch of cookies has just popped out of the oven. (The "real" smoking feature, with its special cinnamon scent, gives it away!) "Elsie's Gingerbread" is the first *North Pole* limited edition and will be produced only through 1998.

Glass Ornament Works . . . "Glass Ornament Works" reveals the site of Santa's secret hobby – making hand-blown glass ornaments! Clusters of ornaments hang from great metal frames shaped like Christmas trees. And as if that weren't enough, practically every corner of the multi-faceted roof is topped with a little gold ornament (just in case you weren't sure what went on inside!)

Mrs. Claus' Greenhouse . . . It's not easy growing flowers at the *North Pole*, but leave it to Mrs. Claus to get the job done! The main building has bright colors and steep angles, while the attached greenhouse tantalizes with hints of red, green and yellow. The real treat for collectors is the greenhouse roof, which is see-through, revealing the colorful, scented treasures inside!

Santa's Light Shop . . . It's not just the curved roof, green spires and quirky porch projection of "Santa's Light Shop" that make it fun to look at, but the bright lights as well: they light up the shop's sign with all the colors of the rainbow! Out front, Christmas trees stand decked out in Santa's latest batch of bulbs. Now if only he could get them to stop blinking . . .

North Pole Accessories . . . In "Delivering The Christmas Greens" (set/2), Mrs. Claus and a trio of elves deliver a selection of healthy fir trees from her greenhouse. Meanwhile, an elf sits slumped against a trunk full of wires and bulbs in "Untangle The Christmas Lights" and three more elves look like they're on the verge of getting into big trouble in "Don't Break The Ornaments" (set/2). *North Pole*'s entry in the *Classic Ornament Series* is "Santa's Lookout Tower."

General Heritage Village

General Heritage Village Accessories . . . The "Village Animated Sledding Hill" and the new "Poinsettia Delivery Truck" make wonderful accessory additions to whichever village you collect.

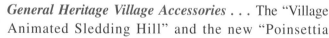

*D*epartment 56 announces Heritage Village retirements each year and for the past several years the list has been published in *USA Today* as well as on the Department 56 website (*www.department56.com*). The following Heritage Village pieces (listed with issue year in parentheses) were retired on November 6, 1997.

Dickens' Village
❑ Dudden Cross Church (1995)
❑ Gad's Hill Place (LE-1997)
❑ Giggelswick Mutton & Ham (1994)
❑ Great Denton Mill (1993)
❑ Hather Harness (1994)
❑ Portobello Road Thatched Cottages (1994, set/3)
  ❑ *Browning Cottage*
  ❑ *Cobb Cottage*
  ❑ *Mr. & Mrs. Pickle*
❑ Tower Of London (1997, set/5)
❑ Wrenbury Shops (1995, set/3) ◊
  ❑ *The Chop Shop*
  ❑ *Wrenbury Baker*

◊ Only two of the three pieces in this set are retired. The other piece, "T. Puddlewick Spectacle Shop," is currently available.

New England Village
❑ Arlington Falls Church (1994)
❑ Blue Star Ice Co. (1993)
❑ Jeremiah Brewster House (1995)
❑ Thomas J. Julian House (1995)

Alpine Village
❑ Apotheke (1986)
❑ E. Staubr Backer (1986)
❑ Grist Mill (1988)
❑ Metterniche Wurst (1992)

Christmas in the City
❑ Brokerage House (1994)
❑ First Metropolitan Bank (1994)
❑ Hollydale's Department Store (1991)
❑ Ivy Terrace Apartments (1995)

North Pole
❑ Beard Barber Shop (1994)
❑ Elfin Snow Cone Works (1994)
❑ North Pole Dolls & Santa's Bear Works (1994, set/3)
❑ Popcorn & Cranberry House (1996)
❑ Tin Soldier Shop (1995)

Great Denton Mill

Blue Star Ice Co.

Metterniche Wurst

First Metropolitan Bank

Elfin Snow Cone Works

*Two Rivers
Bridge*

*Cobbler &
Clock Peddler*

*Blue Star Ice
Harvesters*

*Hot Dog
Vendor*

*Snow Cone
Elves*

General Heritage Village Accessories
- ❏ Churchyard Fence Extensions (1992, set/4)
- ❏ Churchyard Gate & Fence (1992, set/3)
- ❏ The Holly & The Ivy (1997, set/2)
- ❏ Two Rivers Bridge (1994)
- ❏ Village Porcelain Pine, Large (1992)
- ❏ Village Porcelain Pine, Small (1992)
- ❏ Village Porcelain Pine Trees (1994, set/2)

Dickens' Village Accessories
- ❏ Chelsea Market Fish Monger & Cart (1993, set/2)
- ❏ Chelsea Market Fruit Monger & Cart (1993, set/2)
- ❏ "A Christmas Carol" Reading By Charles Dickens (1996, LE-42,500, set/7)
- ❏ Christmas Carol Holiday Trimming Set (1994, set/21)

Dickens' Village Accessories, cont.
- ❏ Cobbler & Clock Peddler (1995, set/2)
- ❏ Gad's Hill Place Ornament (LE-1997)
- ❏ Lionhead Bridge (1992)
- ❏ Thatchers (1994, set/3)
- ❏ Yeomen Of The Guard (1996, set/5)

New England Village Accessories
- ❏ Blue Star Ice Harvesters (1993, set/2)

Christmas in the City Accessories
- ❏ Hot Dog Vendor (1994, set/3)
- ❏ Street Musicians (1993, set/3)

North Pole Accessories
- ❏ Charting Santa's Course (1995, set/2)
- ❏ Snow Cone Elves (1994, set/4)

THEY'RE HISTORY!

Department 56 announced to retailers in early 1998 that they will no longer be publishing the informative "History Lists" for current and retired buildings and accessories that village collectors have come to know and love. Instead, new color brochures will be provided to retailers.

COLLECTOR'S
VALUE GUIDE™

*T*his section highlights the ten most valuable pieces in Heritage Village as determined by their value on the secondary market. In order to qualify for the Top Ten the pieces must have top dollar value and show a significant percentage increase from their original price, as shown by our Market Meter. This year's list includes five pieces from Dickens' Village, two each from New England Village and Christmas in the City and one from Alpine Village.

#1

DICKENS' VILLAGE MILL (LE-2,500)
Dickens' Village, #6519-6
Issued 1985 — Retired 1986
Issue Price: $35
Secondary Market Price: $5,100
Market Meter: +14,471%

This building was the first limited edition produced for *Dickens' Village*, though most people probably did not realize it when they purchased the mill. It was only after the village gained in popularity and people began to try to complete their sets that collectors began to realize what a small amount (only 2,500) of buildings were produced. If you're looking for for "Dickens' Village Mill" be prepared to pay a king's ransom! Also, be sure to examine the piece closely for firing lines and cracks beneath the wheel and in the shed door.

#2

NORMAN CHURCH (LE-3,500)
Dickens' Village, #6502-1
Issued 1986 — Retired 1987
Issue Price: $40
Secondary Market Price: $3,300
Market Meter: +8,150%

Issued in 1986 with a production limit of 3,500, the "Norman Church" was the second limited edition in *Dickens' Village*. The church fit so snugly into its original packaging that many collectors cut or otherwise altered the box so as to be able to remove the church, or to store it, without damaging the piece. As a result, most of the boxes have succumbed to time and wear, and it's very hard to find the piece with the box intact.

#3

CATHEDRAL CHURCH OF ST. MARK (LE-3,024)
Christmas in the City, #5549-2
Issued 1991 — Retired 1993
Issue Price: $120
Secondary Market Price: $2,150
Market Meter: +1,692%

Originally scheduled to be limited to 17,500 pieces, the "Cathedral Church Of St. Mark" had a multitude of production problems. Many of the buildings had cracks, while others arrived at retailers in three pieces. After grappling with the problems for two years, Department 56 decided to stop production. Due to retailer returns, the number of pieces actually in circulation is less than the 3,024 issued.

#4

CHESTERTON MANOR HOUSE (LE-7,500)
Dickens' Village, #6568-4
Issued 1987 — Retired 1988
Issue Price: $45
Secondary Market Price: $1,650
Market Meter: +3,567%

"Chesterton Manor House" was the third limited edition for *Dickens' Village*, and was available for one year. This elegant manor is the epitome of good taste and civilized gentility. Only 7,500 pieces were made, and not all have made it to this day in mint condition. Be sure to check carefully for any firing lines or stress cracks, as they are known to plague this piece. The chimney is quite fragile, and if it was broken in the past it may be reattached

with glue, therefore lowering the secondary market value
of the piece.

**THE ORIGINAL SHOPS OF DICKENS'
VILLAGE (SET/7)**
Dickens' Village, #6515-3
Issued 1984 — Retired 1988
Issue Price: $175
Secondary Market Price: $1,360
Market Meter: +677%

The inaugural set for *Dickens' Village,* these seven
shops paved the way for this popular village. Available
for four years, the shops were retired just as *Dickens'
Village* fever was heating up. Collectors began the
search for this set, and many were surprised to come
across single shops. The decision to sell these buildings
as a set or as individual buildings was made at the retail
level. Some store owners would display a set, and have
each one individually marked for sale. As a result, many
single buildings are available at the secondary market
level, waiting to be reunited with the set once again!

NEW ENGLAND VILLAGE (SET/7)
New England Village, #6530-7
Issued 1986 — Retired 1989
Issue Price: $170
Secondary Market Price: $1,232
Market Meter: +625%

Introduced in 1987, this seven-piece set was the
kick-off for *New England Village.* Available for four
years, "New England Village" had everything you need-

ed to give your town a good start - a general store, a post office, a schoolhouse, a church and more! As with the *Dickens' Village* set, this grouping has been broken up and sold individually on the secondary market, in some instances due to breakage. One interesting thing to note is that the church was also issued by Department 56 as an individual piece with the stock number 6539-0.

#7

SMYTHE WOOLEN MILL (LE-7,500)
New England Village, #6543-9
Issued 1987 — Retired 1988
Issue Price: $42
Secondary Market Price: $1,180
Market Meter: +2,710%

The only limited edition to date in *New England Village*, the "Smythe Woolen Mill" is the second mill to grace the Top Ten. Through the years the mill has appealed to more than just *New England Village* collectors, as *Dickens' Village* enthusiasts have snuck into stores (or secondary market shows) and made purchases to satisfy their own mill-envy!

#8

JOSEF ENGEL FARMHOUSE
Alpine Village, #5952-8
Issued 1987 — Retired 1989
Issue Price: $33
Secondary Market Price: $990
Market Meter: +2,900%

In production for only two years, this farmhouse was the first piece to retire from *Alpine Village*. The rustic charm of "Josef Engel Farmhouse" also appealed to *New England Village* collectors. Pieces in prime condition are especially hard to find, because the many small corners on this piece may have been chipped and nicked over time. Be sure to inspect the stairs as well, as pieces with broken stairs could have been reassembled with glue.

#9

DICKENS' COTTAGES (SET/3)
Dickens' Village, #6518-8
Issued 1985 — Retired 1988
Issue Price: $75
Secondary Market Price: $980
Market Meter: +1,207%

Muted colors and the fact that the three cottages in this set were originally issued without any names almost caused them to be totally overlooked by retailers and collectors. In 1987, the cottages appeared in stores with their identities finally revealed: "Stone Cottage," "Tudor Cottage" and "Thatched Cottage." The "Stone Cottage" comes in two colors, the most common being green. If you find one of these sets with a tan "Stone Cottage," expect to pay more for it.

#10

PALACE THEATRE
Christmas in the City, #5963-3
Issued 1987 — Retired 1989
Issue Price: $45
Secondary Market Price: $960
Market Meter: +2,033%

If you love theater, you might think it fitting that the "Palace Theatre" finishes up the Top Ten. But actually, this piece from *Christmas in the City* got into the #10 position because of a secondary market rush caused by a rumor. The building was retired in 1989, and reports that a shipment never made it to retailers started a rush to buy among collectors, therefore driving up the secondary market price. Fraught with production problems right from the start, the "Palace Theatre" consistently suffered from concave walls, bulges, and breakage.

How To Use Your Value Guide

Ashbury Inn
Issued: 1991 • Retired: 1995
#5555-7 • Original Price: $55
Market Value: $80

1. Locate your piece in the value guide. This section lists the entire Heritage Village Collection and is arranged by village in the following order: *Dickens' Village, New England Village, Alpine Village, Christmas in the City, North Pole, Disney Parks Village Series* and *Little Town Of Bethlehem.* Buildings are listed first, followed by a separate section of accessories. The Value Guide is organized alphabetically within each section. Pieces that belong to a set are listed immediately following the set. For example, "Stone Cottage" can be found right after its set, "Dickens' Cottages" on page 36. Alphabetical and numerical indexes can be found in the back of the book.

2. Find the market value of your piece. Variations and their values are listed in parenthesis following the original piece's market value. Pieces for which secondary market pricing is not established are listed as "N/E."

3. Record the year you purchased the piece, the original price that you paid and the current value of the piece in the corresponding boxes at the bottom of the page.

DICKENS' VILLAGE		
Year Purchased	Price Paid	Value of My Collection
1.		
2.		
3.		
4.		
5.		
PENCIL TOTALS		

4. Calculate the value for the page by adding all of the boxes in each column. Use a pencil so you can change the totals as your collection grows!

5. Transfer the totals from each page to the "Total Value Of My Collection" worksheets on pages 106 and 107.

6. Add all of the totals together to determine the overall value of your collection.

Dickens' Village

FACT FILE

Number of Buildings: 113
Year of First Issue: 1984
Current: 28
Retired: 85
Most Valuable: "Dickens' Village Mill" ($5,100)
New For 1998: 9

1

Ashbury Inn
Issued: 1991 • Retired: 1995
#5555-7 • Original Price: $55
Market Value: $80

2
New

Ashwick Lane Hose & Ladder
Issued: 1997 • Current
#58305 • Original Price: $54
Market Value: $54

3
a   b

Barley Bree (set/2)
Issued: 1987 • Retired: 1989
#5900-5 • Original Price: $60
Market Value: $410

3a

Barn
Issued: 1987 • Retired: 1989
#5900-5 • Original Price: $30
Market Value: N/E

3b

Farmhouse
Issued: 1987 • Retired: 1989
#5900-5 • Original Price: $30
Market Value: N/E

DICKENS' VILLAGE

	Year Purchased	Price Paid	Value of My Collection
1.			
2.			
3.			
3a.			
3b.			
PENCIL TOTALS			

4

Barmby Moor Cottage
Issued: 1997 • Current
#58324 • Original Price: $48
Market Value: $48

5

Bishops Oast House
Issued: 1990 • Retired: 1992
#5567-0 • Original Price: $45
Market Value: $82

6

Blenham Street Bank
Issued: 1995 • Current
#58330 • Original Price: $60
Market Value: $60

7

Version 2

Blythe Pond Mill House
Issued: 1986 • Retired: 1990
#6508-0 • Original Price: $37
Market Value: $305
("By The Pond" – $142)

8

Boarding & Lodging School
("18", LE-1993)
Charles Dickens' Signature Series
Issued: 1993 • Retired: 1993
#5809-2 • Original Price: $48
Market Value: $181

9

Boarding & Lodging School ("43")
Issued: 1994 • Current
#5810-6 • Original Price: $48
Market Value: $48

Dickens' Village

	Year Purchased	Price Paid	Value of My Collection
4.			
5.			
6.			
7.			
8.			
9.			
10.			
PENCIL TOTALS			

10

Brick Abbey
Issued: 1987 • Retired: 1989
#6549-8 • Original Price: $33
Market Value: $390

(11)

Butter Tub Barn
Issued: 1996 • Current
#58338 • Original Price: $48
Market Value: $48

(12)

Butter Tub Farmhouse
Issued: 1996 • Current
#58337 • Original Price: $40
Market Value: $40

(13)

C. Fletcher Public House (LE-12,500)
Issued: 1988 • Retired: 1989
#5904-8 • Original Price: $35
Market Value: $575

(14)

Chadbury Station And Train
Issued: 1986 • Retired: 1989
#6528-5 • Original Price: $65
Market Value: $400

(15)

Chesterton Manor House (LE-7,500)
Issued: 1987 • Retired: 1988
#6568-4 • Original Price: $45
Market Value: $1,650

(16)

Christmas Carol Cottage
(with magic smoking element)
Christmas Carol Revisited
Issued: 1996 • Current
#58339 • Original Price: $60
Market Value: $60

(17)

a *b* *c*

Christmas Carol Cottages (set/3)
Issued: 1986 • Retired: 1995
#6500-5 • Original Price: $75
Market Value: $135

DICKENS' VILLAGE BUILDINGS

DICKENS' VILLAGE

	Year Purchased	Price Paid	Value of My Collection
11.			
12.			
13.			
14.			
15.			
16.			
17.			
PENCIL TOTALS			

Value Guide — Heritage Village Buildings

17a

The Cottage Of Bob Cratchit & Tiny Tim
Issued: 1986 • Retired: 1995
#6500-5 • Original Price: $25
Market Value: $70

17b

Fezziwig's Warehouse
Issued: 1986 • Retired: 1995
#6500-5 • Original Price: $25
Market Value: $42

17c

Scrooge & Marley Counting House
Issued: 1986 • Retired: 1995
#6500-5 • Original Price: $25
Market Value: $55

18

Cobblestone Shops (set/3)
Issued: 1988 • Retired: 1990
#5924-2 • Original Price: $95
Market Value: $395

18a

Booter And Cobbler
Issued: 1988 • Retired: 1990
#5924-2 • Original Price: $32
Market Value: $132

18b

T. Wells Fruit & Spice Shop
Issued: 1988 • Retired: 1990
#5924-2 • Original Price: $32
Market Value: $103

DICKENS' VILLAGE

	Year Purchased	Price Paid	Value of My Collection
17a.			
17b.			
17c.			
18.			
18a.			
18b.			
18c.			
✏ PENCIL TOTALS			

18c

The Wool Shop
Issued: 1988 • Retired: 1990
#5924-2 • Original Price: $32
Market Value: $195

DICKENS' VILLAGE BUILDINGS

19

Cobles Police Station
Issued: 1989 • Retired: 1991
#5583-2 • Original Price: $37.50
Market Value: $154

20

Counting House & Silas Thimbleton Barrister
Issued: 1988 • Retired: 1990
#5902-1 • Original Price: $32
Market Value: $93

21
New

Crooked Fence Cottage
Issued: 1997 • Current
#58304 • Original Price: $60
Market Value: $60

22

Crown & Cricket Inn (LE-1992)
Charles Dickens' Signature Series
Issued: 1992 • Retired: 1992
#5750-9 • Original Price: $100
Market Value: $182

23
a
b
c

David Copperfield (set/3)
Issued: 1989 • Retired: 1992
#5550-6 • Original Price: $125
Market Value: $262
(with Peggotty's version 2 – $188)

23a

Betsy Trotwood's Cottage
Issued: 1989 • Retired: 1992
#5550-6 • Original Price: $42.50
Market Value: $68

23b

Mr. Wickfield Solicitor
Issued: 1989 • Retired: 1992
#5550-6 • Original Price: $42.50
Market Value: $100

DICKENS' VILLAGE

	Year Purchased	Price Paid	Value of My Collection
19.			
20.			
21.			
22.			
23.			
23a.			
23b.			
✏ PENCIL TOTALS			

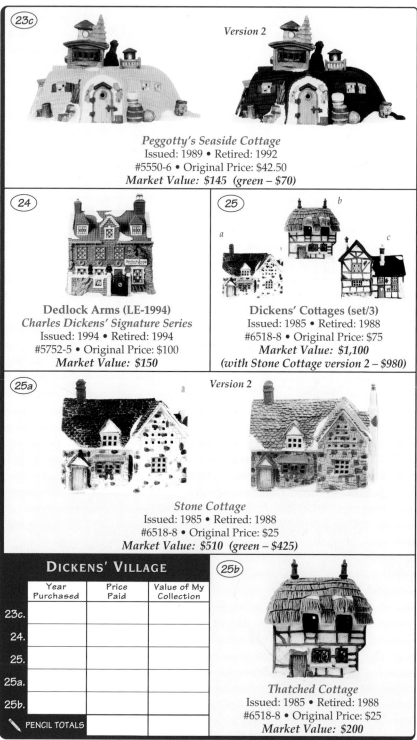

(23c)

Version 2

Peggotty's Seaside Cottage
Issued: 1989 • Retired: 1992
#5550-6 • Original Price: $42.50
Market Value: $145 (green – $70)

(24)

Dedlock Arms (LE-1994)
Charles Dickens' Signature Series
Issued: 1994 • Retired: 1994
#5752-5 • Original Price: $100
Market Value: $150

(25)

a *b* *c*

Dickens' Cottages (set/3)
Issued: 1985 • Retired: 1988
#6518-8 • Original Price: $75
Market Value: $1,100
(with Stone Cottage version 2 – $980)

(25a)

Version 2

Stone Cottage
Issued: 1985 • Retired: 1988
#6518-8 • Original Price: $25
Market Value: $510 (green – $425)

DICKENS' VILLAGE

	Year Purchased	Price Paid	Value of My Collection
23c.			
24.			
25.			
25a.			
25b.			
✏ PENCIL TOTALS			

(25b)

Thatched Cottage
Issued: 1985 • Retired: 1988
#6518-8 • Original Price: $25
Market Value: $200

25c
Tudor Cottage
Issued: 1985 • Retired: 1988
#6518-8 • Original Price: $25
Market Value: $422

26
Dickens' Lane Shops (set/3)
Issued: 1986 • Retired: 1989
#6507-2 • Original Price: $80
Market Value: $638

26a
Cottage Toy Shop
Issued: 1986 • Retired: 1989
#6507-2 • Original Price: $27
Market Value: $245

26b
Thomas Kersey Coffee House
Issued: 1986 • Retired: 1989
#6507-2 • Original Price: $27
Market Value: $185

26c
Tuttle's Pub
Issued: 1986 • Retired: 1989
#6507-2 • Original Price: $27
Market Value: $240

DICKENS' VILLAGE
BUILDINGS

DICKENS' VILLAGE

	Year Purchased	Price Paid	Value of My Collection
25c.			
26.			
26a.			
26b.			
26c.			
PENCIL TOTALS			

27 Version 2 — Version 3 — Version 4 — Version 5

Dickens' Village Church
Issued: 1985 • Retired: 1989
#6516-1 • Original Price: $35
Market Value: $415 (cream – $292, green – $350, tan – $195, butterscotch – $179)

28

Dickens' Village Mill (LE-2,500)
Issued: 1985 • Retired: 1986
#6519-6 • Original Price: $35
Market Value: $5,100

29 Old East Rectory — Sudbury Church

The Spirit Of Giving

Dickens' Village Start A Tradition Set (set/13, Event Piece)
Issued: 1997 • Current
#58322 • Original Price: $75
Market Value: $100

30

Dudden Cross Church
Issued: 1995 • Retired: 1997
#5834-3 • Original Price: $45
Market Value: $50

31

Dursley Manor
Issued: 1995 • Current
#58329 • Original Price: $50
Market Value: $55

DICKENS' VILLAGE

	Year Purchased	Price Paid	Value of My Collection
27.			
28.			
29.			
30.			
31.			
32.			
✎ PENCIL TOTALS			

32 New

East Indies Trading Co.
Issued: 1997 • Current
#58302 • Original Price: $65
Market Value: $65

(33)

Fagin's Hide-A-Way
Issued: 1991 • Retired: 1995
#5552-2 • Original Price: $68
Market Value: $93

(34) Version 2

The Flat Of Ebenezer Scrooge
Issued: 1989 • Current
#5587-5 • Original Price: $37.50
Market Value: $37.50 (no panes – N/E)

(35)

Gad's Hill Place (LE-1997)
Charles Dickens' Signature Series
Issued: 1997 • Retired: 1997
#57535 • Original Price: $98
Market Value: $110

(36)

Giggelswick Mutton & Ham
Issued: 1994 • Retired: 1997
#5822-0 • Original Price: $48
Market Value: $53

(37)

The Grapes Inn (LE-1996)
Charles Dickens' Signature Series
Issued: 1996 • Retired: 1996
#57534 • Original Price: $120
Market Value: $145

(38)

Great Denton Mill
Issued: 1993 • Retired: 1997
#5812-2 • Original Price: $50
Market Value: $58

(39)

Green Gate Cottage (LE-22,500)
Issued: 1989 • Retired: 1990
#5586-7 • Original Price: $65
Market Value: $290

DICKENS' VILLAGE

	Year Purchased	Price Paid	Value of My Collection
33.			
34.			
35.			
36.			
37.			
38.			
39.			
PENCIL TOTALS			

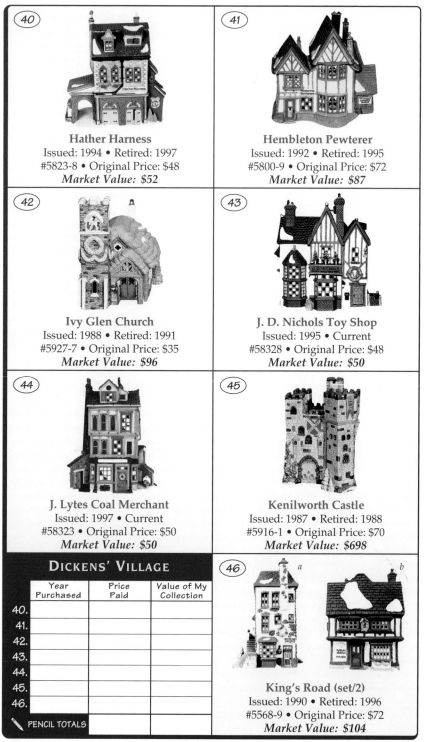

40

Hather Harness
Issued: 1994 • Retired: 1997
#5823-8 • Original Price: $48
Market Value: $52

41

Hembleton Pewterer
Issued: 1992 • Retired: 1995
#5800-9 • Original Price: $72
Market Value: $87

42

Ivy Glen Church
Issued: 1988 • Retired: 1991
#5927-7 • Original Price: $35
Market Value: $96

43

J. D. Nichols Toy Shop
Issued: 1995 • Current
#58328 • Original Price: $48
Market Value: $50

44

J. Lytes Coal Merchant
Issued: 1997 • Current
#58323 • Original Price: $50
Market Value: $50

45

Kenilworth Castle
Issued: 1987 • Retired: 1988
#5916-1 • Original Price: $70
Market Value: $698

DICKENS' VILLAGE

46

a b

King's Road (set/2)
Issued: 1990 • Retired: 1996
#5568-9 • Original Price: $72
Market Value: $104

	Year Purchased	Price Paid	Value of My Collection
40.			
41.			
42.			
43.			
44.			
45.			
46.			
PENCIL TOTALS			

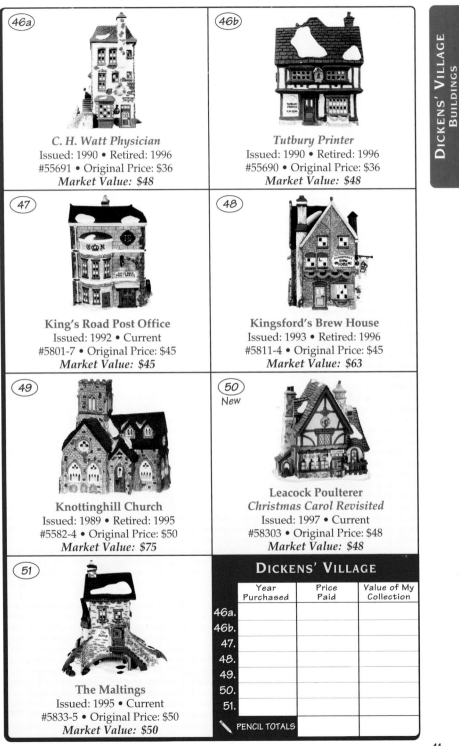

(46a)

C. H. Watt Physician
Issued: 1990 • Retired: 1996
#55691 • Original Price: $36
Market Value: $48

(46b)

Tutbury Printer
Issued: 1990 • Retired: 1996
#55690 • Original Price: $36
Market Value: $48

(47)

King's Road Post Office
Issued: 1992 • Current
#5801-7 • Original Price: $45
Market Value: $45

(48)

Kingsford's Brew House
Issued: 1993 • Retired: 1996
#5811-4 • Original Price: $45
Market Value: $63

(49)

Knottinghill Church
Issued: 1989 • Retired: 1995
#5582-4 • Original Price: $50
Market Value: $75

(50)
New

Leacock Poulterer
Christmas Carol Revisited
Issued: 1997 • Current
#58303 • Original Price: $48
Market Value: $48

(51)

The Maltings
Issued: 1995 • Current
#5833-5 • Original Price: $50
Market Value: $50

DICKENS' VILLAGE

	Year Purchased	Price Paid	Value of My Collection
46a.			
46b.			
47.			
48.			
49.			
50.			
51.			
PENCIL TOTALS			

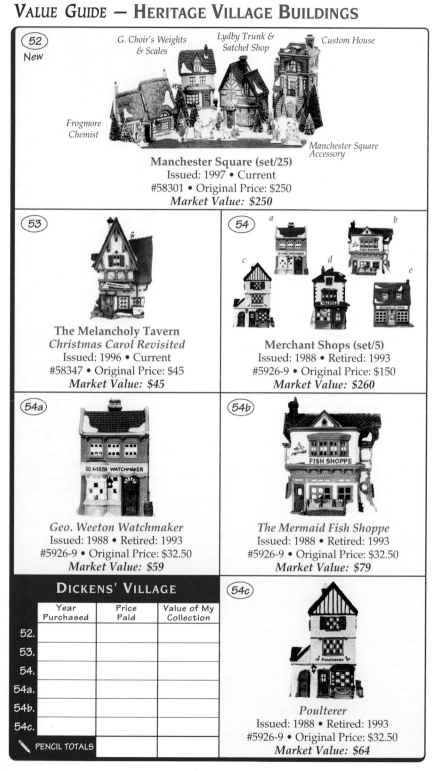

(52) New

G. Choir's Weights & Scales

Lydby Trunk & Satchel Shop

Custom House

Frogmore Chemist

Manchester Square Accessory

Manchester Square (set/25)
Issued: 1997 • Current
#58301 • Original Price: $250
Market Value: $250

(53)

The Melancholy Tavern
Christmas Carol Revisited
Issued: 1996 • Current
#58347 • Original Price: $45
Market Value: $45

(54)

a   b
c   d   e

Merchant Shops (set/5)
Issued: 1988 • Retired: 1993
#5926-9 • Original Price: $150
Market Value: $260

(54a)

Geo. Weeton Watchmaker
Issued: 1988 • Retired: 1993
#5926-9 • Original Price: $32.50
Market Value: $59

(54b)

The Mermaid Fish Shoppe
Issued: 1988 • Retired: 1993
#5926-9 • Original Price: $32.50
Market Value: $79

Dickens' Village

	Year Purchased	Price Paid	Value of My Collection
52.			
53.			
54.			
54a.			
54b.			
54c.			
PENCIL TOTALS			

(54c)

Poulterer
Issued: 1988 • Retired: 1993
#5926-9 • Original Price: $32.50
Market Value: $64

(54d)

Walpole Tailors
Issued: 1988 • Retired: 1993
#5926-9 • Original Price: $32.50
Market Value: $60

(54e)

White Horse Bakery
Issued: 1988 • Retired: 1993
#5926-9 • Original Price: $32.50
Market Value: $70

(55)

Mulberrie Court
Issued: 1996 • Current
#58345 • Original Price: $90
Market Value: $90

(56)

Nephew Fred's Flat
Issued: 1991 • Retired: 1994
#5557-3 • Original Price: $35
Market Value: $82

(57)

Nettie Quinn Puppets & Marionettes
Issued: 1996 • Current
#58344 • Original Price: $50
Market Value: $50

(58)

Nicholas Nickleby (set/2)
Issued: 1988 • Retired: 1991
#5925-0 • Original Price: $72
Market Value: $175
(with Nickleby Cottage version 2 – $204)

(58a) *Version 2*

Nicholas Nickleby Cottage
Issued: 1988 • Retired: 1991
#5925-0 • Original Price: $36
Market Value: $92 ("Nickolas" – $127)

DICKENS' VILLAGE

	Year Purchased	Price Paid	Value of My Collection
54d.			
54e.			
55.			
56.			
57.			
58.			
58a.			
PENCIL TOTALS			

DICKENS' VILLAGE
BUILDINGS

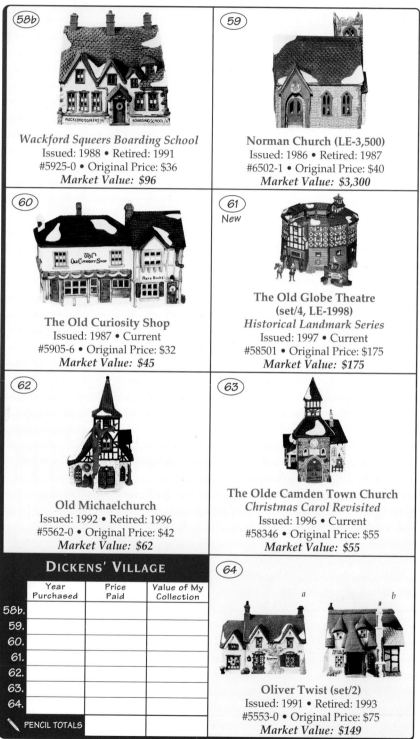

58b

Wackford Squeers Boarding School
Issued: 1988 • Retired: 1991
#5925-0 • Original Price: $36
Market Value: $96

59

Norman Church (LE-3,500)
Issued: 1986 • Retired: 1987
#6502-1 • Original Price: $40
Market Value: $3,300

60

The Old Curiosity Shop
Issued: 1987 • Current
#5905-6 • Original Price: $32
Market Value: $45

61
New

The Old Globe Theatre
(set/4, LE-1998)
Historical Landmark Series
Issued: 1997 • Current
#58501 • Original Price: $175
Market Value: $175

62

Old Michaelchurch
Issued: 1992 • Retired: 1996
#5562-0 • Original Price: $42
Market Value: $62

63

The Olde Camden Town Church
Christmas Carol Revisited
Issued: 1996 • Current
#58346 • Original Price: $55
Market Value: $55

Dickens' Village

	Year Purchased	Price Paid	Value of My Collection
58b.			
59.			
60.			
61.			
62.			
63.			
64.			
PENCIL TOTALS			

64

a *b*

Oliver Twist (set/2)
Issued: 1991 • Retired: 1993
#5553-0 • Original Price: $75
Market Value: $149

(64a)

Brownlow House
Issued: 1991 • Retired: 1993
#5553-0 • Original Price: $37.50
Market Value: $83

(64b)

Maylie Cottage
Issued: 1991 • Retired: 1993
#5553-0 • Original Price: $37.50
Market Value: $70

(65)

a *b* *c* *d* *e* *f* *g*

The Original Shops Of Dickens' Village (set/7)
Issued: 1984 • Retired: 1988
#6515-3 • Original Price: $175
Market Value: $1,360

(65a)

Abel Beesley Butcher
Issued: 1984 • Retired: 1988
#6515-3 • Original Price: $25
Market Value: $138

(65b)

Bean And Son Smithy Shop
Issued: 1984 • Retired: 1988
#6515-3 • Original Price: $25
Market Value: $203

(65c)

Candle Shop
Issued: 1984 • Retired: 1988
#6515-3 • Original Price: $25
Market Value: $210

DICKENS' VILLAGE

	Year Purchased	Price Paid	Value of My Collection
64a.			
64b.			
65.			
65a.			
65b.			
65c.			
✎ PENCIL TOTALS			

DICKENS' VILLAGE
BUILDINGS

65d

Crowntree Inn
Issued: 1984 • Retired: 1988
#6515-3 • Original Price: $25
Market Value: $319

65e

Golden Swan Baker
Issued: 1984 • Retired: 1988
#6515-3 • Original Price: $25
Market Value: $188

65f

Green Grocer
Issued: 1984 • Retired: 1988
#6515-3 • Original Price: $25
Market Value: $205

65g

Jones & Co. Brush & Basket Shop
Issued: 1984 • Retired: 1988
#6515-3 • Original Price: $25
Market Value: $310

66

The Pied Bull Inn (LE-1993)
Charles Dickens' Signature Series
Issued: 1993 • Retired: 1993
#5751-7 • Original Price: $100
Market Value: $160

67

Portobello Road Thatched
Cottages (set/3)
Issued: 1994 • Retired: 1997
#5824-6 • Original Price: $120
Market Value: $128

DICKENS' VILLAGE

	Year Purchased	Price Paid	Value of My Collection
65d.			
65e.			
65f.			
65g.			
66.			
67.			
67a.			
✏ PENCIL TOTALS			

67a

Browning Cottage
Issued: 1994 • Retired: 1997
#58249 • Original Price: $40
Market Value: $43

67b

Cobb Cottage
Issued: 1994 • Retired: 1997
#58248 • Original Price: $40
Market Value: $43

67c

Mr. & Mrs. Pickle
Issued: 1994 • Retired: 1997
#58247 • Original Price: $40
Market Value: $43

68

a   *b*   *c*

Pump Lane Shoppes (set/3)
Issued: 1993 • Retired: 1996
#5808-4 • Original Price: $112
Market Value: $142

68a

Bumpstead Nye Cloaks & Canes
Issued: 1993 • Retired: 1996
#58085 • Original Price: $37.50
Market Value: $48

68b

Lomas Ltd. Molasses
Issued: 1993 • Retired: 1996
#58086 • Original Price: $37.50
Market Value: $48

68c

W.M. Wheat Cakes & Puddings
Issued: 1993 • Retired: 1996
#58087 • Original Price: $37.50
Market Value: $48

69

Quilly's Antiques
Issued: 1996 • Current
#58348 • Original Price: $46
Market Value: $46

DICKENS' VILLAGE

	Year Purchased	Price Paid	Value of My Collection
67b.			
67c.			
68.			
68a.			
68b.			
68c.			
69.			
PENCIL TOTALS			

DICKENS' VILLAGE BUILDINGS

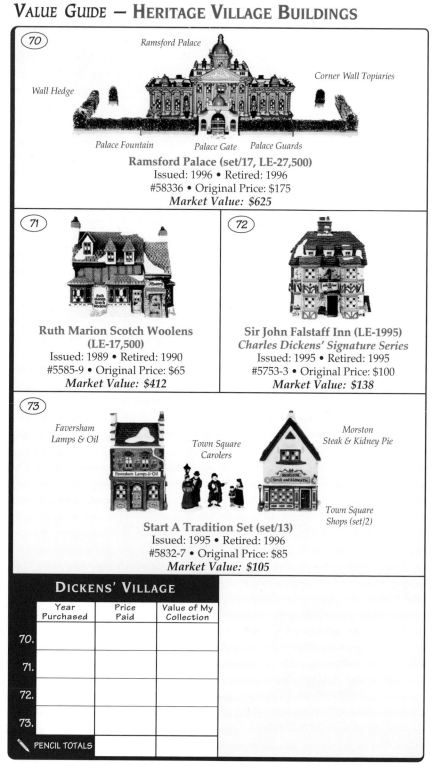

70

Ramsford Palace

Corner Wall Topiaries

Wall Hedge

Palace Fountain   Palace Gate   Palace Guards

Ramsford Palace (set/17, LE-27,500)
Issued: 1996 • Retired: 1996
#58336 • Original Price: $175
Market Value: $625

71

Ruth Marion Scotch Woolens (LE-17,500)
Issued: 1989 • Retired: 1990
#5585-9 • Original Price: $65
Market Value: $412

72

Sir John Falstaff Inn (LE-1995)
Charles Dickens' Signature Series
Issued: 1995 • Retired: 1995
#5753-3 • Original Price: $100
Market Value: $138

73

Faversham
Lamps & Oil

Town Square
Carolers

Morston
Steak & Kidney Pie

Town Square
Shops (set/2)

Start A Tradition Set (set/13)
Issued: 1995 • Retired: 1996
#5832-7 • Original Price: $85
Market Value: $105

Dickens' Village

	Year Purchased	Price Paid	Value of My Collection
70.			
71.			
72.			
73.			
PENCIL TOTALS			

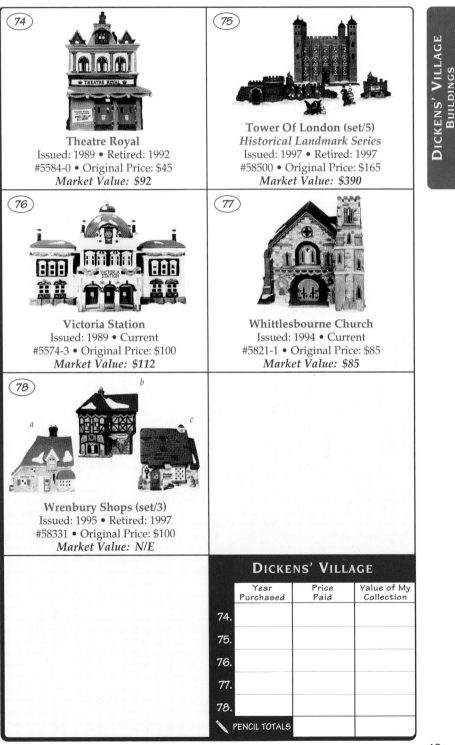

(74)

Theatre Royal
Issued: 1989 • Retired: 1992
#5584-0 • Original Price: $45
Market Value: $92

(75)

Tower Of London (set/5)
Historical Landmark Series
Issued: 1997 • Retired: 1997
#58500 • Original Price: $165
Market Value: $390

(76)

Victoria Station
Issued: 1989 • Current
#5574-3 • Original Price: $100
Market Value: $112

(77)

Whittlesbourne Church
Issued: 1994 • Current
#5821-1 • Original Price: $85
Market Value: $85

(78)

Wrenbury Shops (set/3)
Issued: 1995 • Retired: 1997
#58331 • Original Price: $100
Market Value: N/E

Dickens' Village

	Year Purchased	Price Paid	Value of My Collection
74.			
75.			
76.			
77.			
78.			
PENCIL TOTALS			

(78a)

The Chop Shop
Issued: 1995 • Retired: 1997
#58333 • Original Price: $35
Market Value: $40

(78b)

T. Puddlewick Spectacle Shop
Issued: 1995 • Current
#58334 • Original Price: $35
Market Value: $35

(78c)

Wrenbury Baker
Issued: 1995 • Retired: 1997
#58332 • Original Price: $35
Market Value: $40

New England Village

FACT FILE
Number of Buildings: 51
Year of First Issue: 1986
Current: 14
Retired: 37
Most Valuable: "New England Village" (set/7, $1,315)
New For 1998: 3

DICKENS' VILLAGE

	Year Purchased	Price Paid	Value of My Collection
78a.			
78b.			
78c.			

NEW ENGLAND VILLAGE

1.			
PENCIL TOTALS			

(1)

a   *b*

A. Bieler Farm (set/2)
Issued: 1993 • Retired: 1996
#5648-0 • Original Price: $92
Market Value: $120

VALUE GUIDE – HERITAGE VILLAGE BUILDINGS

1a

Pennsylvania Dutch Barn
Issued: 1993 • Retired: 1996
#56482 • Original Price: $50
Market Value: $65

1b

Pennsylvania Dutch Farmhouse
Issued: 1993 • Retired: 1996
#56481 • Original Price: $42
Market Value: $62

2

Version 2   Version 3

Ada's Bed And Boarding House
Issued: 1988 • Retired: 1991
#5940-4 • Original Price: $36
*Market Value: $320 (pale yellow/rear steps part of mold – $170,
pale yellow/rear steps attached separately – $136)*

3

Apple Valley School
Issued: 1996 • Current
#56172 • Original Price: $35
Market Value: $35

4

Arlington Falls Church
Issued: 1994 • Retired: 1997
#5651-0 • Original Price: $40
Market Value: $44

NEW ENGLAND VILLAGE

	Year Purchased	Price Paid	Value of My Collection
1a.			
1b.			
2.			
3.			
4.			
PENCIL TOTALS			

51

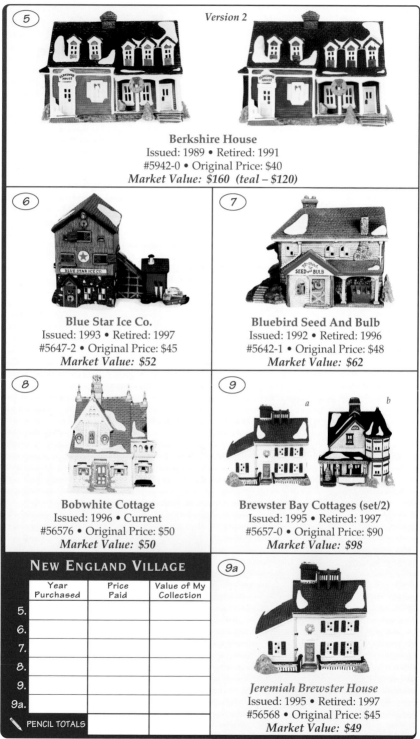

⑤

Version 2

Berkshire House
Issued: 1989 • Retired: 1991
#5942-0 • Original Price: $40
Market Value: $160 (teal – $120)

⑥

Blue Star Ice Co.
Issued: 1993 • Retired: 1997
#5647-2 • Original Price: $45
Market Value: $52

⑦

Bluebird Seed And Bulb
Issued: 1992 • Retired: 1996
#5642-1 • Original Price: $48
Market Value: $62

⑧

Bobwhite Cottage
Issued: 1996 • Current
#56576 • Original Price: $50
Market Value: $50

⑨

a   *b*

Brewster Bay Cottages (set/2)
Issued: 1995 • Retired: 1997
#5657-0 • Original Price: $90
Market Value: $98

New England Village

⑨a

	Year Purchased	Price Paid	Value of My Collection
5.			
6.			
7.			
8.			
9.			
9a.			
✎ PENCIL TOTALS			

Jeremiah Brewster House
Issued: 1995 • Retired: 1997
#56568 • Original Price: $45
Market Value: $49

(9b)

Thomas T. Julian House
Issued: 1995 • Retired: 1997
#56569 • Original Price: $45
Market Value: $49

(10)

Cape Keag Fish Cannery
Issued: 1994 • Current
#5652-9 • Original Price: $48
Market Value: $48

(11)

Captain's Cottage
Issued: 1990 • Retired: 1996
#5947-1 • Original Price: $40
Market Value: $58

(12)

Cherry Lane Shops (set/3)
Issued: 1988 • Retired: 1990
#5939-0 • Original Price: $80
Market Value: $360

(12a)

Anne Shaw Toys
Issued: 1988 • Retired: 1990
#5939-0 • Original Price: $27
Market Value: $177

(12b)

Ben's Barbershop
Issued: 1988 • Retired: 1990
#5939-0 • Original Price: $27
Market Value: $118

(12c)

Otis Hayes Butcher Shop
Issued: 1988 • Retired: 1990
#5939-0 • Original Price: $27
Market Value: $92

NEW ENGLAND VILLAGE BUILDINGS

NEW ENGLAND VILLAGE

	Year Purchased	Price Paid	Value of My Collection
9b.			
10.			
11.			
12.			
12a.			
12b.			
12c.			
PENCIL TOTALS			

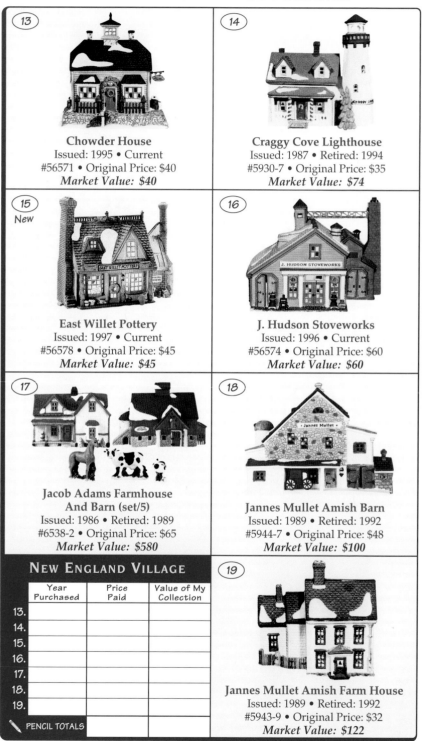

13

Chowder House
Issued: 1995 • Current
#56571 • Original Price: $40
Market Value: $40

14

Craggy Cove Lighthouse
Issued: 1987 • Retired: 1994
#5930-7 • Original Price: $35
Market Value: $74

15
New

East Willet Pottery
Issued: 1997 • Current
#56578 • Original Price: $45
Market Value: $45

16

J. Hudson Stoveworks
Issued: 1996 • Current
#56574 • Original Price: $60
Market Value: $60

17

**Jacob Adams Farmhouse
And Barn (set/5)**
Issued: 1986 • Retired: 1989
#6538-2 • Original Price: $65
Market Value: $580

18

Jannes Mullet Amish Barn
Issued: 1989 • Retired: 1992
#5944-7 • Original Price: $48
Market Value: $100

New England Village

	Year Purchased	Price Paid	Value of My Collection
13.			
14.			
15.			
16.			
17.			
18.			
19.			
PENCIL TOTALS			

19

Jannes Mullet Amish Farm House
Issued: 1989 • Retired: 1992
#5943-9 • Original Price: $32
Market Value: $122

20

McGrebe-Cutters & Sleighs
Issued: 1991 • Retired: 1995
#5640-5 • Original Price: $45
Market Value: $70

21

Navigational Charts & Maps
Issued: 1996 • Current
#56575 • Original Price: $48
Market Value: $48

22

a *b* *c*
d *e* *f* *g*

New England Village (set/7)
Issued: 1986 • Retired: 1989
#6530-7 • Original Price: $170
Market Value: $1,315 (with Steeple Church version 2 – $1,232)

22a

Apothecary Shop
Issued: 1986 • Retired: 1989
#6530-7 • Original Price: $25
Market Value: $116

22b

Brick Town Hall
Issued: 1986 • Retired: 1989
#6530-7 • Original Price: $25
Market Value: $220

22c

General Store
Issued: 1986 • Retired: 1989
#6530-7 • Original Price: $25
Market Value: $360

New England Village

	Year Purchased	Price Paid	Value of My Collection
20.			
21.			
22.			
22a.			
22b.			
22c.			
PENCIL TOTALS			

22d

Livery Stable & Boot Shop
Issued: 1986 • Retired: 1989
#6530-7 • Original Price: $25
Market Value: $160

22e

Nathaniel Bingham Fabrics
Issued: 1986 • Retired: 1989
#6530-7 • Original Price: $25
Market Value: $177

22f

Red Schoolhouse
Issued: 1986 • Retired: 1989
#6530-7 • Original Price: $25
Market Value: $276

22g Version 2

Steeple Church
Issued: 1986 • Retired: 1989
#6530-7 • Original Price: $25
Market Value: $193
(tree attached with glue – $110)

23

Old North Church
Issued: 1988 • Current
#5932-3 • Original Price: $40
Market Value: $48

24

Pierce Boat Works
Issued: 1995 • Current
#56573 • Original Price: $55
Market Value: $55

New England Village

	Year Purchased	Price Paid	Value of My Collection
22d.			
22e.			
22f.			
22g.			
23.			
24.			
25.			
PENCIL TOTALS			

25

Pigeonhead Lighthouse
Issued: 1994 • Current
#5653-7 • Original Price: $50
Market Value: $50

26
New

Semple's Smokehouse
Issued: 1997 • Current
#56580 • Original Price: $45
Market Value: $45

27

Shingle Creek House
Issued: 1990 • Retired: 1994
#5946-3 • Original Price: $37.50
Market Value: $65

28
a *b* *c*

Sleepy Hollow (set/3)
Issued: 1990 • Retired: 1993
#5954-4 • Original Price: $96
Market Value: $199

28a

Ichabod Crane's Cottage
Issued: 1990 • Retired: 1993
#5954-4 • Original Price: $32
Market Value: $65

28b

Sleepy Hollow School
Issued: 1990 • Retired: 1993
#5954-4 • Original Price: $32
Market Value: $104

28c

Van Tassel Manor
Issued: 1990 • Retired: 1993
#5954-4 • Original Price: $32
Market Value: $70

29

Sleepy Hollow Church
Issued: 1990 • Retired: 1993
#5955-2 • Original Price: $36
Market Value: $70

NEW ENGLAND VILLAGE
BUILDINGS

NEW ENGLAND VILLAGE

	Year Purchased	Price Paid	Value of My Collection
26.			
27.			
28.			
28a.			
28b.			
28c.			
29.			
PENCIL TOTALS			

(30)

Smythe Woolen Mill (LE-7,500)
Issued: 1987 • Retired: 1988
#6543-9 • Original Price: $42
Market Value: $1,180

(31)
New

Steen's Maple House
(with magic smoking element)
Issued: 1997 • Current
#56579 • Original Price: $60
Market Value: $60

(32)

Steeple Church
Issued: 1986 • Retired: 1990
#6539-0 • Original Price: $30
Market Value: $102

(33)

Stoney Brook Town Hall
Issued: 1992 • Retired: 1995
#5644-8 • Original Price: $42
Market Value: $68

(34)

Timber Knoll Log Cabin
Issued: 1987 • Retired: 1990
#6544-7 • Original Price: $28
Market Value: $185

(35)

Van Guilder's Ornamental Ironworks
Issued: 1997 • Current
#56577 • Original Price: $50
Market Value: $50

New England Village

	Year Purchased	Price Paid	Value of My Collection
30.			
31.			
32.			
33.			
34.			
35.			
36.			
✏ PENCIL TOTALS			

(36)

Weston Train Station
Issued: 1987 • Retired: 1989
#5931-5 • Original Price: $42
Market Value: $294

(37)

Woodbridge Post Office
Issued: 1995 • Current
#56572 • Original Price: $40
Market Value: $40

(38)

Yankee Jud Bell Casting
Issued: 1992 • Retired: 1995
#5643-0 • Original Price: $44
Market Value: $66

Alpine Village

FACT FILE
Number of Buildings: 18
Year of First Issue: 1986
Current: 8
Retired: 10
Most Valuable: "Josef Engel Farmhouse" ($990)
New For 1998: 1

(1)

Version 2

Alpine Church
Issued: 1987 • Retired: 1991
#6541-2 • Original Price: $32
Market Value: $410 (brown trim – $174)

(2)

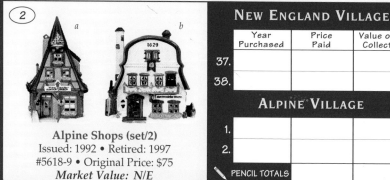

a   *b*

Alpine Shops (set/2)
Issued: 1992 • Retired: 1997
#5618-9 • Original Price: $75
Market Value: N/E

NEW ENGLAND VILLAGE

	Year Purchased	Price Paid	Value of My Collection
37.			
38.			

ALPINE VILLAGE

1.			
2.			
PENCIL TOTALS			

2a

Kukuck Uhren
Issued: 1992 • Current
#56191 • Original Price: $37.50
Market Value: $37.50

2b

Metterniche Wurst
Issued: 1992 • Retired: 1997
#56190 • Original Price: $37.50
Market Value: $40

3

Alpine Village (set/5)
Issued: 1986 • Retired: 1996
#6540-4 • Original Price: $150
Market Value: $183

3a

Apotheke
Issued: 1986 • Retired: 1997
#65407 • Original Price: $25
Market Value: $42

3b

Besson Bierkeller
Issued: 1986 • Retired: 1996
#65405 • Original Price: $25
Market Value: $50

3c

E. Staubr Backer
Issued: 1986 • Retired: 1997
#65408 • Original Price: $25
Market Value: $42

Alpine Village

	Year Purchased	Price Paid	Value of My Collection
2a.			
2b.			
3.			
3a.			
3b.			
3c.			
3d.			
PENCIL TOTALS			

3d

Gasthof Eisl
Issued: 1986 • Retired: 1996
#65406 • Original Price: $25
Market Value: $50

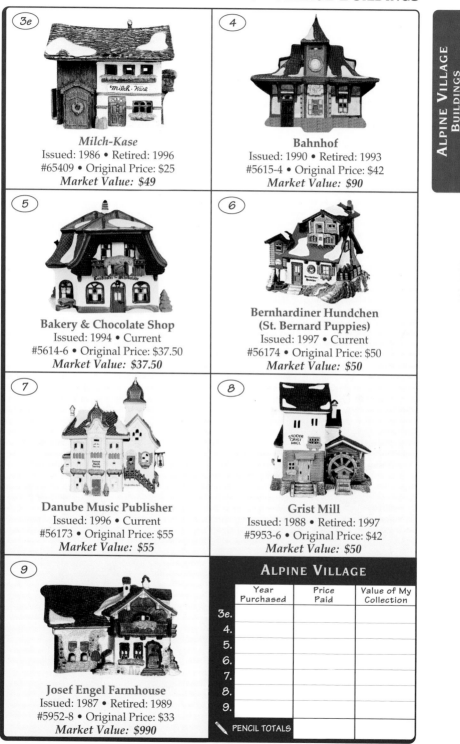

3e

Milch-Kase
Issued: 1986 • Retired: 1996
#65409 • Original Price: $25
Market Value: $49

4

Bahnhof
Issued: 1990 • Retired: 1993
#5615-4 • Original Price: $42
Market Value: $90

5

Bakery & Chocolate Shop
Issued: 1994 • Current
#5614-6 • Original Price: $37.50
Market Value: $37.50

6

**Bernhardiner Hundchen
(St. Bernard Puppies)**
Issued: 1997 • Current
#56174 • Original Price: $50
Market Value: $50

7

Danube Music Publisher
Issued: 1996 • Current
#56173 • Original Price: $55
Market Value: $55

8

Grist Mill
Issued: 1988 • Retired: 1997
#5953-6 • Original Price: $42
Market Value: $50

9

Josef Engel Farmhouse
Issued: 1987 • Retired: 1989
#5952-8 • Original Price: $33
Market Value: $990

ALPINE VILLAGE

	Year Purchased	Price Paid	Value of My Collection
3e.			
4.			
5.			
6.			
7.			
8.			
9.			
PENCIL TOTALS			

ALPINE VILLAGE
BUILDINGS

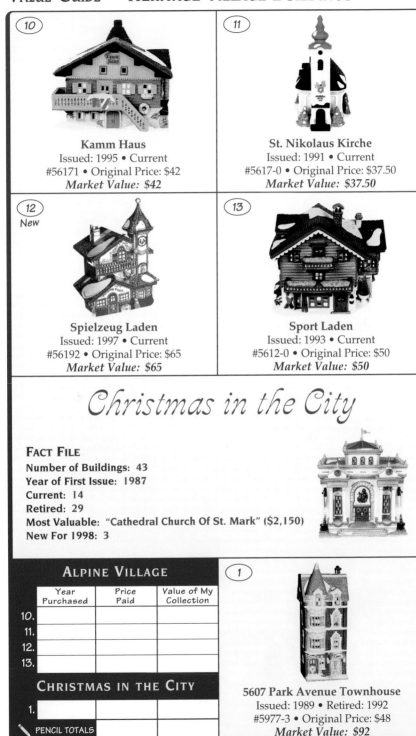

10

Kamm Haus
Issued: 1995 • Current
#56171 • Original Price: $42
Market Value: $42

11

St. Nikolaus Kirche
Issued: 1991 • Current
#5617-0 • Original Price: $37.50
Market Value: $37.50

12
New

Spielzeug Laden
Issued: 1997 • Current
#56192 • Original Price: $65
Market Value: $65

13

Sport Laden
Issued: 1993 • Current
#5612-0 • Original Price: $50
Market Value: $50

Christmas in the City

FACT FILE
Number of Buildings: 43
Year of First Issue: 1987
Current: 14
Retired: 29
Most Valuable: "Cathedral Church Of St. Mark" ($2,150)
New For 1998: 3

ALPINE VILLAGE

	Year Purchased	Price Paid	Value of My Collection
10.			
11.			
12.			
13.			

CHRISTMAS IN THE CITY

1.		
PENCIL TOTALS		

1

5607 Park Avenue Townhouse
Issued: 1989 • Retired: 1992
#5977-3 • Original Price: $48
Market Value: $92

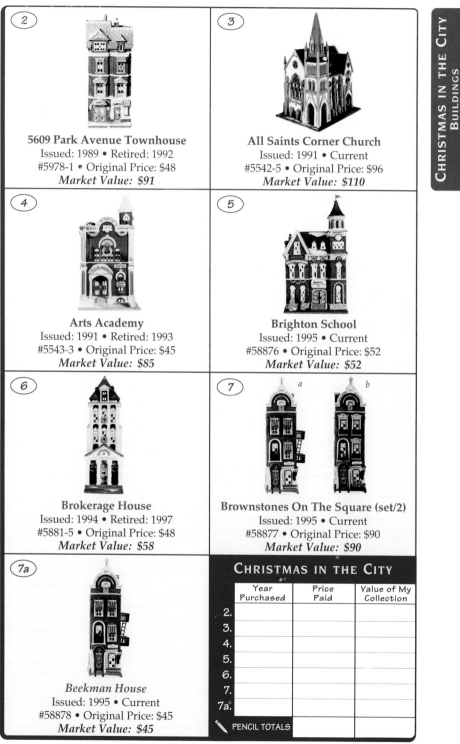

2

5609 Park Avenue Townhouse
Issued: 1989 • Retired: 1992
#5978-1 • Original Price: $48
Market Value: $91

3

All Saints Corner Church
Issued: 1991 • Current
#5542-5 • Original Price: $96
Market Value: $110

4

Arts Academy
Issued: 1991 • Retired: 1993
#5543-3 • Original Price: $45
Market Value: $85

5

Brighton School
Issued: 1995 • Current
#58876 • Original Price: $52
Market Value: $52

6

Brokerage House
Issued: 1994 • Retired: 1997
#5881-5 • Original Price: $48
Market Value: $58

7

a   *b*

Brownstones On The Square (set/2)
Issued: 1995 • Current
#58877 • Original Price: $90
Market Value: $90

7a

Beekman House
Issued: 1995 • Current
#58878 • Original Price: $45
Market Value: $45

CHRISTMAS IN THE CITY

	Year Purchased	Price Paid	Value of My Collection
2.			
3.			
4.			
5.			
6.			
7.			
7a.			
✏ PENCIL TOTALS			

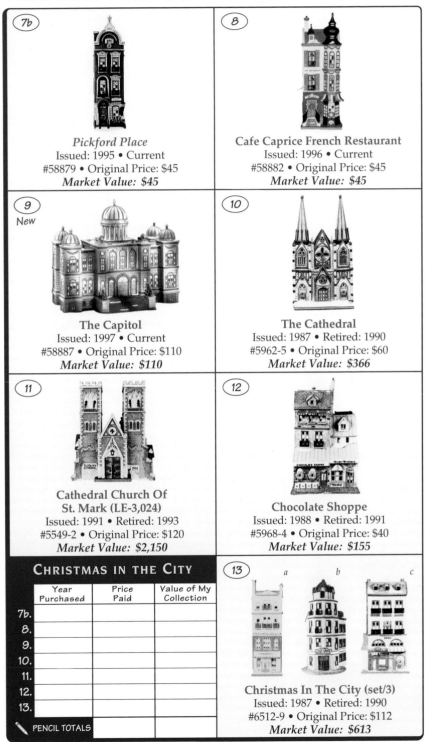

7b

Pickford Place
Issued: 1995 • Current
#58879 • Original Price: $45
Market Value: $45

8

Cafe Caprice French Restaurant
Issued: 1996 • Current
#58882 • Original Price: $45
Market Value: $45

9
New

The Capitol
Issued: 1997 • Current
#58887 • Original Price: $110
Market Value: $110

10

The Cathedral
Issued: 1987 • Retired: 1990
#5962-5 • Original Price: $60
Market Value: $366

11

Cathedral Church Of
St. Mark (LE-3,024)
Issued: 1991 • Retired: 1993
#5549-2 • Original Price: $120
Market Value: $2,150

12

Chocolate Shoppe
Issued: 1988 • Retired: 1991
#5968-4 • Original Price: $40
Market Value: $155

CHRISTMAS IN THE CITY

	Year Purchased	Price Paid	Value of My Collection
7b.			
8.			
9.			
10.			
11.			
12.			
13.			
✏ PENCIL TOTALS			

13   a   b   c

Christmas In The City (set/3)
Issued: 1987 • Retired: 1990
#6512-9 • Original Price: $112
Market Value: $613

13a

Bakery
Issued: 1987 • Retired: 1990
#6512-9 • Original Price: $37.50
Market Value: $122

13b

Tower Restaurant
Issued: 1987 • Retired: 1990
#6512-9 • Original Price: $37.50
Market Value: $260

13c

Toy Shop And Pet Store
Issued: 1987 • Retired: 1990
#6512-9 • Original Price: $37.50
Market Value: $260

14

The City Globe
Issued: 1997 • Current
#58883 • Original Price: $65
Market Value: $65

15

City Hall
Issued: 1988 • Retired: 1991
#5969-2 • Original Price: $65
Market Value: $187

16

The Doctor's Office
Issued: 1991 • Retired: 1994
#5544-1 • Original Price: $60
Market Value: $86

17

Dorothy's Dress Shop (LE-12,500)
Issued: 1989 • Retired: 1991
#5974-9 • Original Price: $70
Market Value: $395

CHRISTMAS IN THE CITY

	Year Purchased	Price Paid	Value of My Collection
13a.			
13b.			
13c.			
14.			
15.			
16.			
17.			
✎ PENCIL TOTALS			

18

First Metropolitan Bank
Issued: 1994 • Retired: 1997
#5882-3 • Original Price: $60
Market Value: $68

19

Grand Central Railway Station
Issued: 1996 • Current
#58881 • Original Price: $90
Market Value: $90

20

Hank's Market
Issued: 1988 • Retired: 1992
#5970-6 • Original Price: $40
Market Value: $90

21

Heritage Museum Of Art
Issued: 1994 • Current
#5883-1 • Original Price: $96
Market Value: $96

22

Hi-De-Ho Nightclub
Issued: 1997 • Current
#58884 • Original Price: $52
Market Value: $52

23

Hollydale's Department Store
Issued: 1991 • Retired: 1997
#5534-4 • Original Price: $75
Market Value: $95

CHRISTMAS IN THE CITY

	Year Purchased	Price Paid	Value of My Collection
18.			
19.			
20.			
21.			
22.			
23.			
24.			
PENCIL TOTALS			

24

Holy Name Church
Issued: 1995 • Current
#58875 • Original Price: $96
Market Value: $96

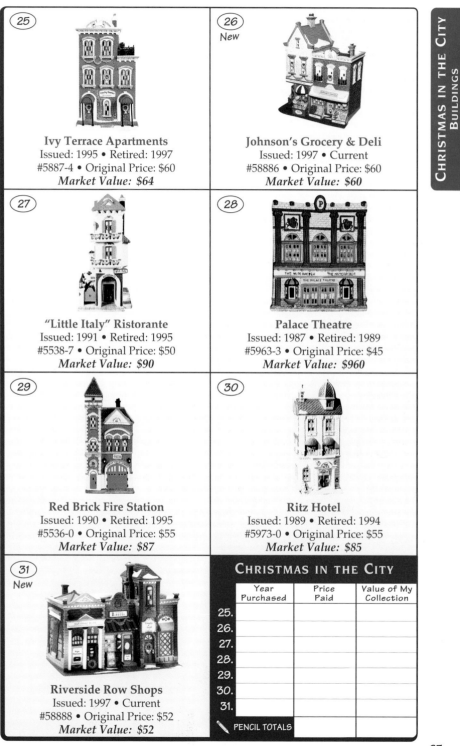

25

Ivy Terrace Apartments
Issued: 1995 • Retired: 1997
#5887-4 • Original Price: $60
Market Value: $64

26
New

Johnson's Grocery & Deli
Issued: 1997 • Current
#58886 • Original Price: $60
Market Value: $60

27

"Little Italy" Ristorante
Issued: 1991 • Retired: 1995
#5538-7 • Original Price: $50
Market Value: $90

28

Palace Theatre
Issued: 1987 • Retired: 1989
#5963-3 • Original Price: $45
Market Value: $960

29

Red Brick Fire Station
Issued: 1990 • Retired: 1995
#5536-0 • Original Price: $55
Market Value: $87

30

Ritz Hotel
Issued: 1989 • Retired: 1994
#5973-0 • Original Price: $55
Market Value: $85

31
New

Riverside Row Shops
Issued: 1997 • Current
#58888 • Original Price: $52
Market Value: $52

CHRISTMAS IN THE CITY

	Year Purchased	Price Paid	Value of My Collection
25.			
26.			
27.			
28.			
29.			
30.			
31.			
PENCIL TOTALS			

CHRISTMAS IN THE CITY
BUILDINGS

(32)

Sutton Place Brownstones
Issued: 1987 • Retired: 1989
#5961-7 • Original Price: $80
Market Value: $925

(33) *a* *b* *c*

Uptown Shoppes (set/3)
Issued: 1992 • Retired: 1996
#5531-0 • Original Price: $150
Market Value: $186

(33a)

City Clockworks
Issued: 1992 • Retired: 1996
#55313 • Original Price: $56
Market Value: $70

(33b)

Haberdashery
Issued: 1992 • Retired: 1996
#55311 • Original Price: $40
Market Value: $58

(33c)

Music Emporium
Issued: 1992 • Retired: 1996
#55312 • Original Price: $54
Market Value: $70

(34)

Variety Store
Issued: 1988 • Retired: 1990
#5972-2 • Original Price: $45
Market Value: $191

Christmas in the City

	Year Purchased	Price Paid	Value of My Collection
32.			
33.			
33a.			
33b.			
33c.			
34.			
35.			
✎ PENCIL TOTALS			

(35)

Washington Street Post Office
Issued: 1996 • Current
#58880 • Original Price: $52
Market Value: $52

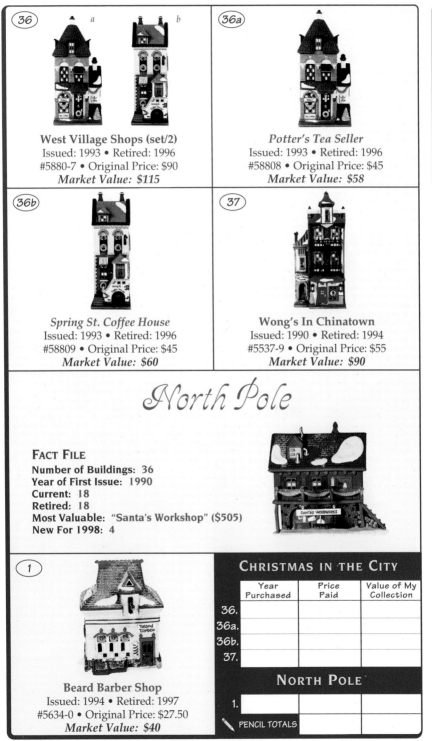

36 *a* *b*

West Village Shops (set/2)
Issued: 1993 • Retired: 1996
#5880-7 • Original Price: $90
Market Value: $115

36a

Potter's Tea Seller
Issued: 1993 • Retired: 1996
#58808 • Original Price: $45
Market Value: $58

36b

Spring St. Coffee House
Issued: 1993 • Retired: 1996
#58809 • Original Price: $45
Market Value: $60

37

Wong's In Chinatown
Issued: 1990 • Retired: 1994
#5537-9 • Original Price: $55
Market Value: $90

North Pole

FACT FILE
Number of Buildings: 36
Year of First Issue: 1990
Current: 18
Retired: 18
Most Valuable: "Santa's Workshop" ($505)
New For 1998: 4

1

Beard Barber Shop
Issued: 1994 • Retired: 1997
#5634-0 • Original Price: $27.50
Market Value: $40

CHRISTMAS IN THE CITY

	Year Purchased	Price Paid	Value of My Collection
36.			
36a.			
36b.			
37.			

NORTH POLE

1.			
PENCIL TOTALS			

Value Guide – Heritage Village Buildings

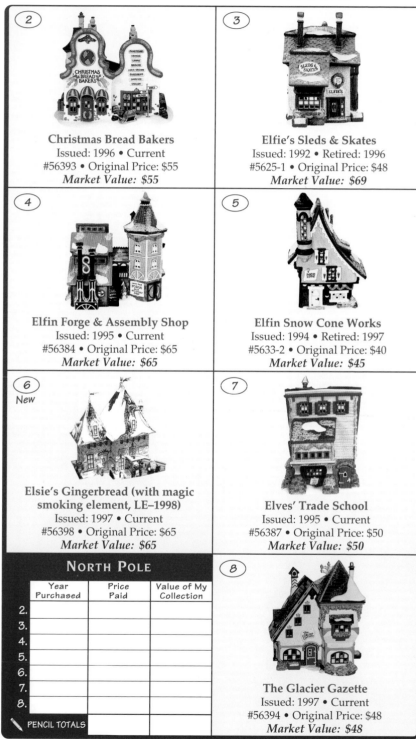

2

Christmas Bread Bakers
Issued: 1996 • Current
#56393 • Original Price: $55
Market Value: $55

3

Elfie's Sleds & Skates
Issued: 1992 • Retired: 1996
#5625-1 • Original Price: $48
Market Value: $69

4

Elfin Forge & Assembly Shop
Issued: 1995 • Current
#56384 • Original Price: $65
Market Value: $65

5

Elfin Snow Cone Works
Issued: 1994 • Retired: 1997
#5633-2 • Original Price: $40
Market Value: $45

6
New

Elsie's Gingerbread (with magic smoking element, LE–1998)
Issued: 1997 • Current
#56398 • Original Price: $65
Market Value: $65

7

Elves' Trade School
Issued: 1995 • Current
#56387 • Original Price: $50
Market Value: $50

North Pole

	Year Purchased	Price Paid	Value of My Collection
2.			
3.			
4.			
5.			
6.			
7.			
8.			
PENCIL TOTALS			

8

The Glacier Gazette
Issued: 1997 • Current
#56394 • Original Price: $48
Market Value: $48

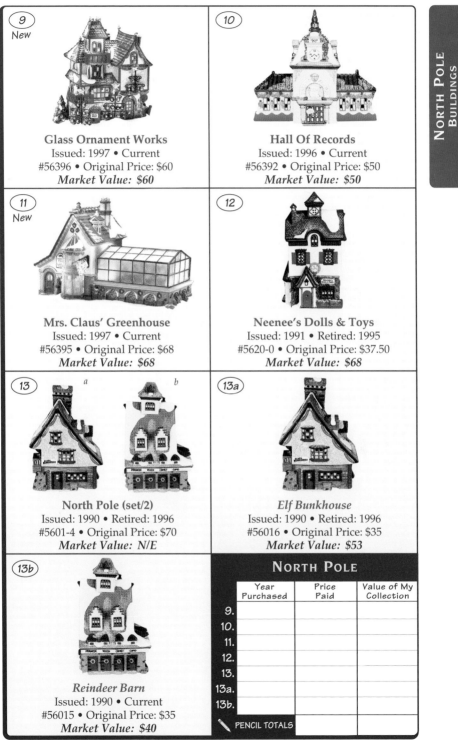

9
New

Glass Ornament Works
Issued: 1997 • Current
#56396 • Original Price: $60
Market Value: $60

10

Hall Of Records
Issued: 1996 • Current
#56392 • Original Price: $50
Market Value: $50

11
New

Mrs. Claus' Greenhouse
Issued: 1997 • Current
#56395 • Original Price: $68
Market Value: $68

12

Neenee's Dolls & Toys
Issued: 1991 • Retired: 1995
#5620-0 • Original Price: $37.50
Market Value: $68

13
a   b

North Pole (set/2)
Issued: 1990 • Retired: 1996
#5601-4 • Original Price: $70
Market Value: N/E

13a

Elf Bunkhouse
Issued: 1990 • Retired: 1996
#56016 • Original Price: $35
Market Value: $53

13b

Reindeer Barn
Issued: 1990 • Current
#56015 • Original Price: $35
Market Value: $40

NORTH POLE

	Year Purchased	Price Paid	Value of My Collection
9.			
10.			
11.			
12.			
13.			
13a.			
13b.			
PENCIL TOTALS			

(14)

North Pole Chapel
Issued: 1993 • Current
#5626-0 • Original Price: $45
Market Value: $45

(15)

North Pole Dolls

Santa's Bear Works

Entrance

North Pole Dolls & Santa's Bear Works (set/3)
Issued: 1994 • Retired: 1997
#5635-9 • Original Price: $96
Market Value: $100

(16)

North Pole Express Depot
Issued: 1993 • Current
#5627-8 • Original Price: $48
Market Value: $48

(17)

a   b

North Pole Shops (set/2)
Issued: 1991 • Retired: 1995
#5621-9 • Original Price: $75
Market Value: $136

(17a)

Orly's Bell & Harness Supply
Issued: 1991 • Retired: 1995
#5621-9 • Original Price: $37.50
Market Value: $70

(17b)

Rimpy's Bakery
Issued: 1991 • Retired: 1995
#5621-9 • Original Price: $37.50
Market Value: $75

North Pole

	Year Purchased	Price Paid	Value of My Collection
14.			
15.			
16.			
17.			
17a.			
17b.			
18.			
✏ PENCIL TOTALS			

(18)

Obbie's Books & Letrinka's Candy
Issued: 1992 • Retired: 1996
#5624-3 • Original Price: $70
Market Value: $95

19

Popcorn & Cranberry House
Issued: 1996 • Retired: 1997
#56388 • Original Price: $45
Market Value: $70

20

Post Office
Issued: 1992 • Current
#5623-5 • Original Price: $45
Market Value: $50

21

**Route 1, North Pole,
Home Of Mr. & Mrs. Claus**
Issued: 1996 • Current
#56391 • Original Price: $110
Market Value: $110

22

Santa's Bell Repair
Issued: 1996 • Current
#56389 • Original Price: $45
Market Value: $45

23
New

Santa's Light Shop
Issued: 1997 • Current
#56397 • Original Price: $52
Market Value: $52

24

Santa's Lookout Tower
Issued: 1993 • Current
#5629-4 • Original Price: $45
Market Value: $48

25

Santa's Rooming House
Issued: 1995 • Current
#56386 • Original Price: $50
Market Value: $50

NORTH POLE

	Year Purchased	Price Paid	Value of My Collection
19.			
20.			
21.			
22.			
23.			
24.			
25.			
PENCIL TOTALS			

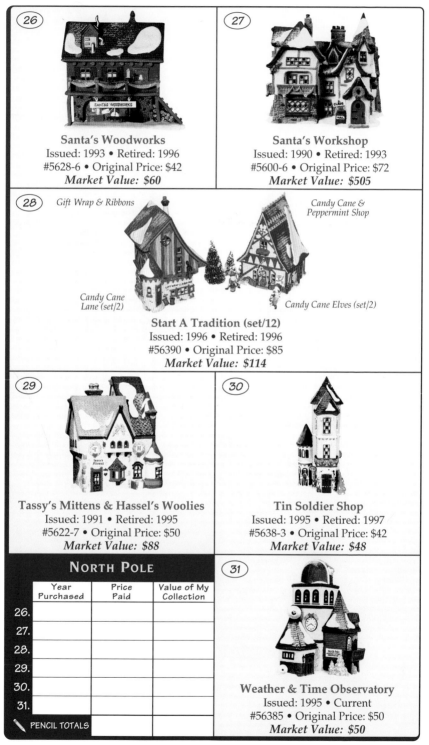

26

Santa's Woodworks
Issued: 1993 • Retired: 1996
#5628-6 • Original Price: $42
Market Value: $60

27

Santa's Workshop
Issued: 1990 • Retired: 1993
#5600-6 • Original Price: $72
Market Value: $505

28

Gift Wrap & Ribbons

Candy Cane &
Peppermint Shop

Candy Cane
Lane (set/2)

Candy Cane Elves (set/2)

Start A Tradition (set/12)
Issued: 1996 • Retired: 1996
#56390 • Original Price: $85
Market Value: $114

29

Tassy's Mittens & Hassel's Woolies
Issued: 1991 • Retired: 1995
#5622-7 • Original Price: $50
Market Value: $88

30

Tin Soldier Shop
Issued: 1995 • Retired: 1997
#5638-3 • Original Price: $42
Market Value: $48

North Pole

	Year Purchased	Price Paid	Value of My Collection
26.			
27.			
28.			
29.			
30.			
31.			
PENCIL TOTALS			

31

Weather & Time Observatory
Issued: 1995 • Current
#56385 • Original Price: $50
Market Value: $50

Disney Parks Village Series

FACT FILE

Number of Buildings: 6
Year of First Issue: 1994
Current: 0
Retired: 6
Most Valuable: "Tinker Bell's Treasures" ($280)
New For 1998: 0

① Disneyland Fire Department #105
Issued: 1994 • Retired: 1996
#5352-0 • Original Price: $45
Market Value: $50

② *Version 2*

Mickey's Christmas Carol (set/2)
Issued: 1994 • Retired: 1996
#5350-3 • Original Price: $144
Market Value: $165
(without spires on dormers – $165)

③ *a* *b*

Olde World Antiques Shops (set/2)
Issued: 1994 • Retired: 1996
#5351-1 • Original Price: $90
Market Value: $100

③a Olde World Antiques I
Issued: 1994 • Retired: 1996
#5351-1 • Original Price: $45
Market Value: $55

③b Olde World Antiques II
Issued: 1994 • Retired: 1996
#5351-1 • Original Price: $45
Market Value: $55

DISNEY PARKS VILLAGE SERIES

	Year Purchased	Price Paid	Value of My Collection
1.			
2.			
3.			
3a.			
3b.			
PENCIL TOTALS			

④

Silversmith
Issued: 1995 • Retired: 1996
#53521 • Original Price: $50
Market Value: $275

⑤

Tinker Bell's Treasures
Issued: 1995 • Retired: 1996
#53522 • Original Price: $60
Market Value: $280

Little Town Of Bethlehem

FACT FILE
Number of Pieces: 12
Year of First Issue: 1987
Current: 12
Retired: 0
Most Valuable: N/A
New For 1998: 0

①

Little Town Of Bethlehem (set/12)
Issued: 1987 • Current
#5975-7 • Original Price: $150
Market Value: $150

DISNEY PARKS VILLAGE SERIES

	Year Purchased	Price Paid	Value of My Collection
4.			
5.			

LITTLE TOWN OF BETHLEHEM

1.			
✏ PENCIL TOTALS			

Test your knowledge of Heritage Village facts here! To check your score, see page 107.

1. *Dickens' Village* is inspired by the 19th century London of author Charles Dickens. Who was the ruler of England when Dickens' novel "Great Expectations" was published in 1861?

2. What show is listed on the marquee as playing at the "Palace Theatre" in *Christmas in the City*?

3. "The Old Globe Theatre" is Department 56's rendition of what the theater may have looked like if it had survived until Charles Dickens' time. According to historians, how did the original Globe Theatre meet its demise in 1613?

4. Heritage Village contains six train stations. Can you name them?

5. During the Christmas of 1818, a church in Austria was left without music because mice had damaged the pipe organ. Father Josef Mohr wrote a poem and organist Franz Gruber put it to music, and thus the Christmas favorite "Silent Night" debuted. What *Alpine Village* building represents the church where this occurred?

6. Seven early *North Pole* pieces featured wreaths with letters on the front of the building. What was Department 56 spelling out?

7. In the *Dickens' Village* accessory "Tallyho!," what activity are the figures engaged in?

8. One building in *New England Village* features a gambrel roof. Which one is it?

9. What was the name of the head of the boarding school in Dickens' novel "Nicholas Nickelby?"

10. In Dickens' time, what was a costermonger?

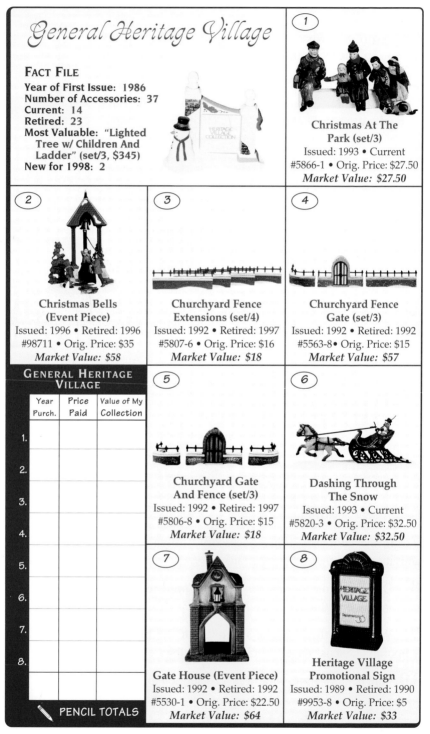

General Heritage Village

FACT FILE
Year of First Issue: 1986
Number of Accessories: 37
Current: 14
Retired: 23
Most Valuable: "Lighted Tree w/ Children And Ladder" (set/3, $345)
New for 1998: 2

1

Christmas At The Park (set/3)
Issued: 1993 • Current
#5866-1 • Orig. Price: $27.50
Market Value: $27.50

2

Christmas Bells (Event Piece)
Issued: 1996 • Retired: 1996
#98711 • Orig. Price: $35
Market Value: $58

3

Churchyard Fence Extensions (set/4)
Issued: 1992 • Retired: 1997
#5807-6 • Orig. Price: $16
Market Value: $18

4

Churchyard Fence Gate (set/3)
Issued: 1992 • Retired: 1992
#5563-8• Orig. Price: $15
Market Value: $57

GENERAL HERITAGE VILLAGE

	Year Purch.	Price Paid	Value of My Collection
1.			
2.			
3.			
4.			
5.			
6.			
7.			
8.			

✎ PENCIL TOTALS

5

Churchyard Gate And Fence (set/3)
Issued: 1992 • Retired: 1997
#5806-8 • Orig. Price: $15
Market Value: $18

6

Dashing Through The Snow
Issued: 1993 • Current
#5820-3 • Orig. Price: $32.50
Market Value: $32.50

7

Gate House (Event Piece)
Issued: 1992 • Retired: 1992
#5530-1 • Orig. Price: $22.50
Market Value: $64

8

Heritage Village Promotional Sign
Issued: 1989 • Retired: 1990
#9953-8 • Orig. Price: $5
Market Value: $33

9

The Holly & The Ivy
(set/2, Event Piece)
Issued: 1997 • Retired: 1997
#56100 • Orig. Price: $17.50
Market Value: $35

10

Lighted Tree w/ Children
And Ladder (set/3)
Issued: 1986 • Retired: 1989
#6510-2 • Orig. Price: $35
Market Value: $345

11

One Horse Open Sleigh
Issued: 1988 • Retired: 1993
#5982-0 • Orig. Price: $20
Market Value: $42

12

Playing In The
Snow (set/3)
Issued: 1993 • Retired: 1996
#5556-5 • Orig. Price: $25
Market Value: $36

13

New

Poinsettia Delivery Truck
Issued: 1997 • Current
#59000 • Orig. Price: $32.50
Market Value: $32.50

14

Porcelain Trees (set/2)
Issued: 1986 • Retired: 1992
#6537-4 • Orig. Price: $14
Market Value: $40

15

Skating Party (set/3)
Issued: 1991 • Current
#5523-9 • Orig. Price: $27.50
Market Value: $27.50

16

Skating Pond
Issued: 1987 • Retired: 1990
#6545-5 • Orig. Price: $24
Market Value: $85

17

Snow Children (set/3)
Issued: 1988 • Retired: 1994
#5938-2 • Orig. Price: $15
Market Value: $34

18

Town Square Gazebo
Issued: 1989 • Retired: 1997
#5513-1 • Orig. Price: $19
Market Value: $19

GENERAL HERITAGE VILLAGE
ACCESSORIES

GENERAL HERITAGE VILLAGE

	Year Purch.	Price Paid	Value of My Collection
9.			
10.			
11.			
12.			
13.			
14.			
15.			
16.			
17.			
18.			

PENCIL TOTALS

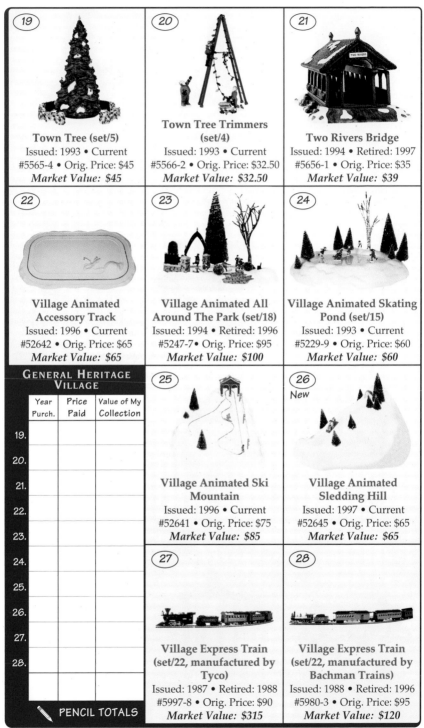

19

Town Tree (set/5)
Issued: 1993 • Current
#5565-4 • Orig. Price: $45
Market Value: $45

20

Town Tree Trimmers (set/4)
Issued: 1993 • Current
#5566-2 • Orig. Price: $32.50
Market Value: $32.50

21

Two Rivers Bridge
Issued: 1994 • Retired: 1997
#5656-1 • Orig. Price: $35
Market Value: $39

22

Village Animated Accessory Track
Issued: 1996 • Current
#52642 • Orig. Price: $65
Market Value: $65

23

Village Animated All Around The Park (set/18)
Issued: 1994 • Retired: 1996
#5247-7• Orig. Price: $95
Market Value: $100

24

Village Animated Skating Pond (set/15)
Issued: 1993 • Current
#5229-9 • Orig. Price: $60
Market Value: $60

General Heritage Village

	Year Purch.	Price Paid	Value of My Collection
19.			
20.			
21.			
22.			
23.			
24.			
25.			
26.			
27.			
28.			

PENCIL TOTALS

25

Village Animated Ski Mountain
Issued: 1996 • Current
#52641 • Orig. Price: $75
Market Value: $85

26

New

Village Animated Sledding Hill
Issued: 1997 • Current
#52645 • Orig. Price: $65
Market Value: $65

27

Village Express Train (set/22, manufactured by Tyco)
Issued: 1987 • Retired: 1988
#5997-8 • Orig. Price: $90
Market Value: $315

28

Village Express Train (set/22, manufactured by Bachman Trains)
Issued: 1988 • Retired: 1996
#5980-3 • Orig. Price: $95
Market Value: $120

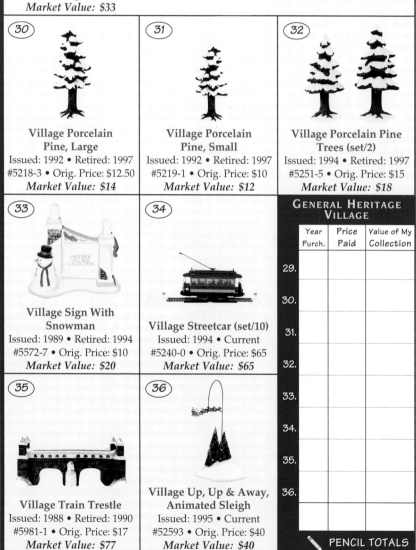

29

Village Express Van
Issued: 1992 • Retired: 1996
#5865-3 • Orig. Price: $25
Market Value: $33

Versions

Black – $151	The Limited Edition – $114
Gold – $1,025	Lock, Stock & Barrel – $135
Bachman's – $92	North Pole City – $70
Bronner's – $65	Parkwest – $500
The Christmas Dove – $65	Robert's – $63
European Imports – $63	St. Nick's – $75
Fortunoff – $136	Stats – $60
Incredible Xmas Place – $85	William Glen – $62
Lemon Tree – $62	The Windsor Shoppe – $60

30

**Village Porcelain
Pine, Large**
Issued: 1992 • Retired: 1997
#5218-3 • Orig. Price: $12.50
Market Value: $14

31

**Village Porcelain
Pine, Small**
Issued: 1992 • Retired: 1997
#5219-1 • Orig. Price: $10
Market Value: $12

32

**Village Porcelain Pine
Trees (set/2)**
Issued: 1994 • Retired: 1997
#5251-5 • Orig. Price: $15
Market Value: $18

33

**Village Sign With
Snowman**
Issued: 1989 • Retired: 1994
#5572-7 • Orig. Price: $10
Market Value: $20

34

Village Streetcar (set/10)
Issued: 1994 • Current
#5240-0 • Orig. Price: $65
Market Value: $65

35

Village Train Trestle
Issued: 1988 • Retired: 1990
#5981-1 • Orig. Price: $17
Market Value: $77

36

**Village Up, Up & Away,
Animated Sleigh**
Issued: 1995 • Current
#52593 • Orig. Price: $40
Market Value: $40

GENERAL HERITAGE VILLAGE

	Year Purch.	Price Paid	Value of My Collection
29.			
30.			
31.			
32.			
33.			
34.			
35.			
36.			
	PENCIL TOTALS		

GENERAL HERITAGE VILLAGE ACCESSORIES

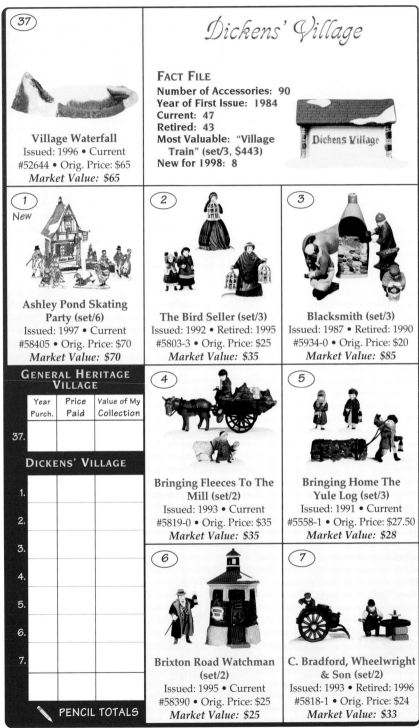

(37)

Village Waterfall
Issued: 1996 • Current
#52644 • Orig. Price: $65
Market Value: $65

Dickens' Village

FACT FILE
Number of Accessories: 90
Year of First Issue: 1984
Current: 47
Retired: 43
Most Valuable: "Village
Train" (set/3, $443)
New for 1998: 8

Dickens Village

(1)
New

Ashley Pond Skating
Party (set/6)
Issued: 1997 • Current
#58405 • Orig. Price: $70
Market Value: $70

(2)

The Bird Seller (set/3)
Issued: 1992 • Retired: 1995
#5803-3 • Orig. Price: $25
Market Value: $35

(3)

Blacksmith (set/3)
Issued: 1987 • Retired: 1990
#5934-0 • Orig. Price: $20
Market Value: $85

GENERAL HERITAGE VILLAGE

	Year Purch.	Price Paid	Value of My Collection
37.			

DICKENS' VILLAGE

1.			
2.			
3.			
4.			
5.			
6.			
7.			

✏ PENCIL TOTALS

(4)

Bringing Fleeces To The
Mill (set/2)
Issued: 1993 • Current
#5819-0 • Orig. Price: $35
Market Value: $35

(5)

Bringing Home The
Yule Log (set/3)
Issued: 1991 • Current
#5558-1 • Orig. Price: $27.50
Market Value: $28

(6)

Brixton Road Watchman
(set/2)
Issued: 1995 • Current
#58390 • Orig. Price: $25
Market Value: $25

(7)

C. Bradford, Wheelwright
& Son (set/2)
Issued: 1993 • Retired: 1996
#5818-1 • Orig. Price: $24
Market Value: $33

⑧ *Version 2*

Carolers (set/3)
Issued: 1984 • Retired: 1990
#6526-9 • Orig. Price: $10
Market Value: $122 (black lamppost – $43)

⑨

Carolers On The Doorstep (set/4)
Issued: 1990 • Retired: 1993
#5570-0 • Orig. Price: $25
Market Value: $46

⑩

Caroling With The Cratchit Family (set/3)
Christmas Carol Revisited
Issued: 1996 • Current
#58396 • Orig. Price: $37.50
Market Value: $37.50

⑪

Chelsea Lane Shoppers (set/4)
Issued: 1993 • Current
#5816-5 • Orig. Price: $30
Market Value: $30

⑫

Chelsea Market Curiosities Monger & Cart (set/2)
Issued: 1994 • Current
#5827-0 • Orig. Price: $27.50
Market Value: $27.50

⑬

Chelsea Market Fish Monger & Cart (set/2)
Issued: 1993 • Retired: 1997
#5814-9 • Orig. Price: $25
Market Value: $30

⑭

Chelsea Market Flower Monger & Cart (set/2)
Issued: 1993 • Current
#5815-7 • Orig. Price: $27.50
Market Value: $27.50

⑮

Chelsea Market Fruit Monger & Cart (set/2)
Issued: 1993 • Retired: 1997
#5813-0 • Orig. Price: $25
Market Value: $35

⑯

Chelsea Market Hat Monger & Cart (set/2)
Issued: 1995 • Current
#58392 • Orig. Price: $27.50
Market Value: $27.50

DICKENS' VILLAGE

	Year Purch.	Price Paid	Value of My Collection
8.			
9.			
10.			
11.			
12.			
13.			
14.			
15.			
16.			

✏ PENCIL TOTALS

DICKENS' VILLAGE ACCESSORIES

(17)

Chelsea Market Mistletoe Monger & Cart (set/2)
Issued: 1994 • Current
#5826-2 • Orig. Price: $25
Market Value: $25

(18)

Childe Pond & Skaters (set/4)
Issued: 1988 • Retired: 1991
#5903-0 • Orig. Price: $30
Market Value: $90

(19)

Christmas Carol Christmas Morning Figures (set/3)
Issued: 1989 • Current
#5588-3 • Orig. Price: $18
Market Value: $18

(20)

Christmas Carol Christmas Spirits Figures (set/4)
Issued: 1989 • Current
#5589-1 • Orig. Price: $27.50
Market Value: $27.50

(21)

Christmas Carol Figures (set/3)
Issued: 1986 • Retired: 1990
#6501-3 • Orig. Price: $12.50
Market Value: $92

(22)

Christmas Carol Holiday Trimming Set (set/21)
Issued: 1994 • Retired: 1997
#5831-9 • Orig. Price: $65
Market Value: $75

DICKENS' VILLAGE

	Year Purch.	Price Paid	Value of My Collection
17.			
18.			
19.			
20.			
21.			
22.			
23.			
24.			
25.			
26.			
✏ PENCIL TOTALS			

(23)

"A Christmas Carol" Reading By Charles Dickens (set/4)
Issued: 1996 • Current
#58403 • Orig. Price: $45
Market Value: $45

(24)

"A Christmas Carol" Reading By Charles Dickens (set/7, LE-42,500)
Charles Dickens' Signature Series
Issued: 1996 • Retired: 1997
#58404 • Orig. Price: $75
Market Value: $150

(25)
New

Christmas Pudding Costermonger (set/3)
Issued: 1997 • Current
#58408 • Orig. Price: $32.50
Market Value: $32.50

(26)

Cobbler & Clock Peddler (set/2)
Issued: 1995 • Retired: 1997
#58394 • Orig. Price: $25
Market Value: $28

27

Come Into The Inn (set/3)
Issued: 1991 • Retired: 1994
#5560-3 • Orig. Price: $22
Market Value: $34

28

Constables (set/3)
Issued: 1989 • Retired: 1991
#5579-4 • Orig. Price: $17.50
Market Value: $70

29

**Crown & Cricket Inn
Ornament (LE-1996)**
Issued: 1996 • Retired: 1996
#98730 • Orig. Price: $15
Market Value: $22

30

**David Copperfield
Characters (set/5)**
Issued: 1989 • Retired: 1992
#5551-4 • Orig. Price: $32.50
Market Value: $46

31

**Dedlock Arms Ornament
(LE-1994)**
Issued: 1994 • Retired: 1994
#9872-8 • Orig. Price: $12.50
Market Value: $24

32

**Delivering Coal For The
Hearth (set/2)**
Issued: 1997 • Current
#58326 • Orig. Price: $32.50
Market Value: $32.50

33
New

Dickens' Village Church
Classic Ornament Series
Issued: 1997 • Current
#98737 • Orig. Price: $15
Market Value: $15

34

Dickens' Village Mill
Classic Ornament Series
Issued: 1997 • Current
#98733 • Orig. Price: $15
Market Value: $15

35

Dickens' Village Sign
Issued: 1987 • Retired: 1993
#6569-2 • Orig. Price: $6
Market Value: $20

**DICKENS' VILLAGE
ACCESSORIES**

DICKENS' VILLAGE

	Year Purch.	Price Paid	Value of My Collection
27.			
28.			
29.			
30.			
31.			
32.			
33.			
34.			
35.			

✏ PENCIL TOTALS

36

Version 2

Dover Coach
Issued: 1987 • Retired: 1990
#6590-0 • Orig. Price: $18
Market Value: $107 (with mustache – $74)

37

Eight Maids A-Milking
(set/2)
*The Twelve Days Of
Dickens' Village*
Issued: 1996 • Current
#58384 • Orig. Price: $25
Market Value: $25

38

English Post Box
Issued: 1992 • Current
#58050 • Orig. Price: $4.50
Market Value: $4.50

39

Farm People & Animals
(set/5)
Issued: 1987 • Retired: 1989
#5901-3 • Orig. Price: $24
Market Value: $107

40
New

Father Christmas's
Journey (track compatible)
Issued: 1997 • Current
#58407 • Orig. Price: $30
Market Value: $30

DICKENS' VILLAGE

	Year Purch.	Price Paid	Value of My Collection
36.			
37.			
38.			
39.			
40.			
41.			
42.			
43.			
44.			

✏ PENCIL TOTALS

41

Fezziwig And Friends
(set/3)
Issued: 1988 • Retired: 1990
#5928-5 • Orig. Price: $12.50
Market Value: $60

42

The Fezziwig Delivery
Wagon
Christmas Carol Revisited
Issued: 1996 • Current
#58400 • Orig. Price: $32.50
Market Value: $32.50

43
New

The Fire Brigade Of
London Town (set/5)
Issued: 1997 • Current
#58406 • Orig. Price: $70
Market Value: $70

44

Five Golden Rings (set/2)
*The Twelve Days Of
Dickens' Village*
Issued: 1995 • Current
#58381 • Orig. Price: $27.50
Market Value: $27.50

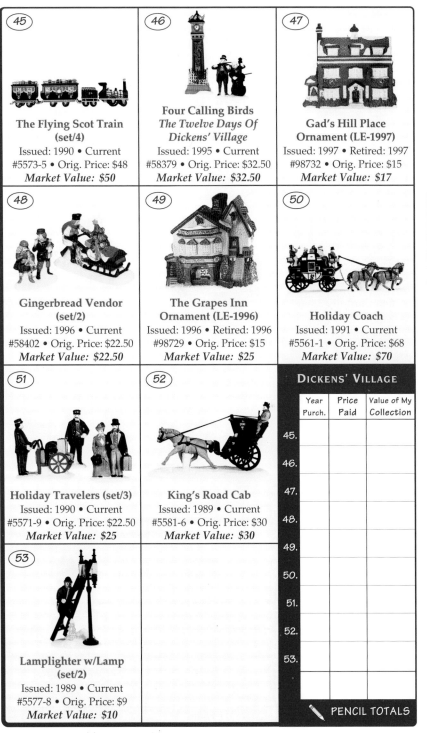

45

The Flying Scot Train (set/4)
Issued: 1990 • Current
#5573-5 • Orig. Price: $48
Market Value: $50

46

Four Calling Birds
The Twelve Days Of Dickens' Village
Issued: 1995 • Current
#58379 • Orig. Price: $32.50
Market Value: $32.50

47

Gad's Hill Place Ornament (LE-1997)
Issued: 1997 • Retired: 1997
#98732 • Orig. Price: $15
Market Value: $17

48

Gingerbread Vendor (set/2)
Issued: 1996 • Current
#58402 • Orig. Price: $22.50
Market Value: $22.50

49

The Grapes Inn Ornament (LE-1996)
Issued: 1996 • Retired: 1996
#98729 • Orig. Price: $15
Market Value: $25

50

Holiday Coach
Issued: 1991 • Current
#5561-1 • Orig. Price: $68
Market Value: $70

51

Holiday Travelers (set/3)
Issued: 1990 • Current
#5571-9 • Orig. Price: $22.50
Market Value: $25

52

King's Road Cab
Issued: 1989 • Current
#5581-6 • Orig. Price: $30
Market Value: $30

53

Lamplighter w/Lamp (set/2)
Issued: 1989 • Current
#5577-8 • Orig. Price: $9
Market Value: $10

DICKENS' VILLAGE ACCESSORIES

DICKENS' VILLAGE

	Year Purch.	Price Paid	Value of My Collection
45.			
46.			
47.			
48.			
49.			
50.			
51.			
52.			
53.			

✏ PENCIL TOTALS

54

Lionhead Bridge
Issued: 1992 • Retired: 1997
#5864-5 • Orig. Price: $22
Market Value: $27

55

**Nicholas Nickleby
Characters (set/4)**
Issued: 1988 • Retired: 1991
#5929-3 • Orig. Price: $20
Market Value: $45

56
New

**Nine Ladies Dancing
(set/2)**
*The Twelve Days Of
Dickens' Village*
Issued: 1997 • Current
#58385 • Orig. Price: $30
Market Value: $30

57
New

Old Curiosity Shop
Classic Ornament Series
Issued: 1997 • Current
#98738 • Orig. Price: $15
Market Value: $15

58

The Old Puppeteer (set/3)
Issued: 1992 • Retired: 1995
#5802-5 • Orig. Price: $32
Market Value: $46

59

**Oliver Twist Characters
(set/3)**
Issued: 1991 • Retired: 1993
#5554-9 • Orig. Price: $35
Market Value: $51

DICKENS' VILLAGE

	Year Purch.	Price Paid	Value of My Collection
54.			
55.			
56.			
57.			
58.			
59.			
60.			
61.			
62.			
✏ PENCIL TOTALS			

60

Version 2

Ox Sled
Issued: 1987 • Retired: 1989
#5951-0 • Orig. Price: $20
Market Value: $263 (blue pants/black seat – $147)

61

A Partridge In A Pear Tree
*The Twelve Days Of
Dickens' Village*
Issued: 1995 • Current
#5835-1 • Orig. Price: $35
Market Value: $35

62

**A Peaceful Glow On
Christmas Eve (set/3)**
Issued: 1994 • Current
#5830-0 • Orig. Price: $30
Market Value: $30

63

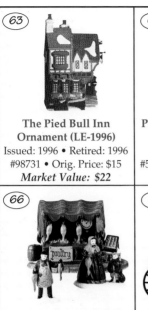

The Pied Bull Inn Ornament (LE-1996)
Issued: 1996 • Retired: 1996
#98731 • Orig. Price: $15
Market Value: $22

64

Portobello Road Peddlers (set/3)
Issued: 1994 • Current
#5828-9 • Orig. Price: $27.50
Market Value: $27.50

65

Postern (Dickens' Village Ten Year Anniversary Piece)
Issued: 1994 • Retired: 1994
#9871-0 • Orig. Price: $17.50
Market Value: $32

66

Poultry Market (set/3)
Issued: 1991 • Retired: 1995
#5559-0 • Orig. Price: $30
Market Value: $46

67

Red Christmas Sulky
Issued: 1996 • Current
#58401 • Orig. Price: $30
Market Value: $30

68

Royal Coach
Issued: 1989 • Retired: 1992
#5578-6 • Orig. Price: $55
Market Value: $85

69

Seven Swans A-Swimming (set/4)
The Twelve Days Of Dickens' Village
Issued: 1996 • Current
#58383 • Orig. Price: $27.50
Market Value: $27.50

70

Shopkeepers (set/4)
Issued: 1987 • Retired: 1988
#5966-8 • Orig. Price: $15
Market Value: $45

71

Silo & Hay Shed (set/2)
Issued: 1987 • Retired: 1989
#5950-1 • Orig. Price: $18
Market Value: $180

72

Sir John Falstaff Inn Ornament (LE-1995)
Issued: 1995 • Retired: 1995
#9870-1 • Orig. Price: $15
Market Value: $22

DICKENS' VILLAGE ACCESSORIES

DICKENS' VILLAGE

	Year Purch.	Price Paid	Value of My Collection
63.			
64.			
65.			
66.			
67.			
68.			
69.			
70.			
71.			
72.			

PENCIL TOTALS

73

Six Geese A-Laying (set/2)
The Twelve Days Of Dickens' Village
Issued: 1995 • Current
#58382 • Orig. Price: $30
Market Value: $30

74

Stone Bridge
Issued: 1987 • Retired: 1990
#6546-3 • Orig. Price: $12
Market Value: $90

75

"Tallyho!" (set/5)
Issued: 1995 • Current
#58391 • Orig. Price: $50
Market Value: $50

76
New

Ten Pipers Piping (set/3)
The Twelve Days Of Dickens' Village
Issued: 1997 • Current
#58386 • Orig. Price: $30
Market Value: $30

77

Tending The New Calves (set/3)
Issued: 1996 • Current
#58395 • Orig. Price: $30
Market Value: $30

78

Thatchers (set/3)
Issued: 1994 • Retired: 1997
#5829-7 • Orig. Price: $35
Market Value: $40

Dickens' Village

	Year Purch.	Price Paid	Value of My Collection
73.			
74.			
75.			
76.			
77.			
78.			
79.			
80.			
81.			
82.			
✏ PENCIL TOTALS			

79

Three French Hens (set/3)
The Twelve Days Of Dickens' Village
Issued: 1995 • Current
#58378 • Orig. Price: $32.50
Market Value: $32.50

80

Town Crier & Chimney Sweep (set/2)
Issued: 1990 • Current
#5569-7 • Orig. Price: $15
Market Value: $16

81

Two Turtle Doves (set/4)
The Twelve Days Of Dickens' Village
Issued: 1995 • Current
#5836-0 • Orig. Price: $32.50
Market Value: $32.50

82

Victoria Station Train Platform
Issued: 1990 • Current
#5575-1 • Orig. Price: $20
Market Value: $22

(83)

Village Street Peddlers (set/2)
Issued: 1992 • Retired: 1994
#5804-1 • Orig. Price: $16
Market Value: $30

(84)

Village Train (set/3)
Issued: 1985 • Retired: 1986
#6527-7 • Orig. Price: $12
Market Value: $443

(85)

Village Well & Holy Cross (set/2)
Issued: 1987 • Retired: 1989
#6547-1 • Orig. Price: $13
Market Value: $165

(86)

Violet Vendor/Carolers/ Chestnut Vendor (set/3)
Issued: 1989 • Retired: 1992
#5580-8 • Orig. Price: $23
Market Value: $46

(87)

Vision Of A Christmas Past (set/3)
Issued: 1993 • Retired: 1996
#5817-3 • Orig. Price: $27.50
Market Value: $38

(88)

Winter Sleighride
Issued: 1994 • Current
#5825-4 • Orig. Price: $18
Market Value: $18

(89)

"Ye Olde Lamplighter" Dickens' Village Sign
Issued: 1995 • Current
#58393 • Orig. Price: $20
Market Value: $20

(90)

Yeomen Of The Guard (set/5)
Issued: 1996 • Retired: 1997
#58397 • Orig. Price: $30
Market Value: $50

DICKENS' VILLAGE ACCESSORIES

DICKENS' VILLAGE

	Year Purch.	Price Paid	Value of My Collection
83.			
84.			
85.			
86.			
87.			
88.			
89.			
90.			

✎ PENCIL TOTALS

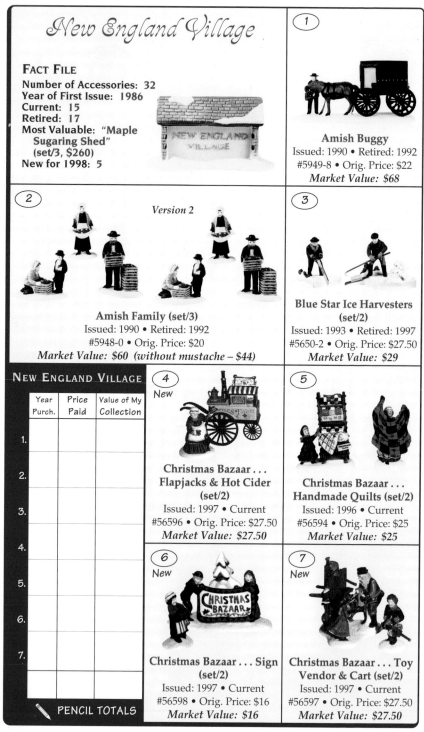

New England Village

FACT FILE
Number of Accessories: 32
Year of First Issue: 1986
Current: 15
Retired: 17
Most Valuable: "Maple Sugaring Shed" (set/3, $260)
New for 1998: 5

①

Amish Buggy
Issued: 1990 • Retired: 1992
#5949-8 • Orig. Price: $22
Market Value: $68

②

Version 2

Amish Family (set/3)
Issued: 1990 • Retired: 1992
#5948-0 • Orig. Price: $20
Market Value: $60 (without mustache – $44)

③

Blue Star Ice Harvesters (set/2)
Issued: 1993 • Retired: 1997
#5650-2 • Orig. Price: $27.50
Market Value: $29

NEW ENGLAND VILLAGE

	Year Purch.	Price Paid	Value of My Collection
1.			
2.			
3.			
4.			
5.			
6.			
7.			

✏ PENCIL TOTALS

④
New

Christmas Bazaar . . . Flapjacks & Hot Cider (set/2)
Issued: 1997 • Current
#56596 • Orig. Price: $27.50
Market Value: $27.50

⑤

Christmas Bazaar . . . Handmade Quilts (set/2)
Issued: 1996 • Current
#56594 • Orig. Price: $25
Market Value: $25

⑥
New

Christmas Bazaar . . . Sign (set/2)
Issued: 1997 • Current
#56598 • Orig. Price: $16
Market Value: $16

⑦
New

Christmas Bazaar . . . Toy Vendor & Cart (set/2)
Issued: 1997 • Current
#56597 • Orig. Price: $27.50
Market Value: $27.50

(8)

Christmas Bazaar . . .
Woolens & Preserves
(set/2)
Issued: 1996 • Current
#56595 • Orig. Price: $25
Market Value: $25

(9)

Covered Wooden Bridge
Issued: 1986 • Retired: 1990
#6531-5 • Orig. Price: $10
Market Value: $43

(10)
New

Craggy Cove Lighthouse
Classic Ornament Series
Issued: 1997 • Current
#98739 • Orig. Price: $15
Market Value: $15

(11)

Farm Animals (set/4)
Issued: 1989 • Retired: 1991
#5945-5 • Orig. Price: $15
Market Value: $46

(12)

Farm Animals (set/8)
Issued: 1995 • Current
#56588 • Orig. Price: $32.50
Market Value: $32.50

(13)

"Fresh Paint" New
England Village Sign
Issued: 1995 • Current
#56592 • Orig. Price: $20
Market Value: $20

(14)

Harvest Pumpkin Wagon
Issued: 1995 • Current
#56591 • Orig. Price: $45
Market Value: $45

(15)

Harvest Seed Cart (set/3)
Issued: 1992 • Retired: 1995
#5645-6 • Orig. Price: $27.50
Market Value: $43

(16)

Knife Grinder (set/2)
Issued: 1993 • Retired: 1996
#5649-9 • Orig. Price: $22.50
Market Value: $30

(17)

Lobster Trappers (set/4)
Issued: 1995 • Current
#56589 • Orig. Price: $35
Market Value: $35

NEW ENGLAND VILLAGE

	Year Purch.	Price Paid	Value of My Collection
8.			
9.			
10.			
11.			
12.			
13.			
14.			
15.			
16.			
17.			

✏ PENCIL TOTALS

NEW ENGLAND VILLAGE
ACCESSORIES

18

Lumberjacks (set/2)
Issued: 1995 • Current
#56590 • Orig. Price: $30
Market Value: $30

19

Maple Sugaring Shed (set/3)
Issued: 1987 • Retired: 1989
#6589-7 • Orig. Price: $19
Market Value: $260

20

Market Day (set/3)
Issued: 1991 • Retired: 1993
#5641-3 • Orig. Price: $35
Market Value: $54

21

New England Village Sign
Issued: 1987 • Retired: 1993
#6570-6 • Orig. Price: $6
Market Value: $20

22

New England Winter Set (set/5)
Issued: 1986 • Retired: 1990
#6532-3 • Orig. Price: $18
Market Value: $52

23

A New Potbellied Stove For Christmas (set/2)
Issued: 1996 • Current
#56593 • Orig. Price: $35
Market Value: $35

NEW ENGLAND VILLAGE

	Year Purch.	Price Paid	Value of My Collection
18.			
19.			
20.			
21.			
22.			
23.			
24.			
25.			
26.			

✏ PENCIL TOTALS

24

The Old Man And The Sea (set/3)
Issued: 1994 • Current
#5655-3 • Orig. Price: $25
Market Value: $25

25

Over The River And Through The Woods
Issued: 1994 • Current
#5654-5 • Orig. Price: $35
Market Value: $35

26

Red Covered Bridge
Issued: 1988 • Retired: 1994
#5987-0 • Orig. Price: $15
Market Value: $30

27

Sleepy Hollow Characters (set/3)
Issued: 1990 • Retired: 1992
#5956-0 • Orig. Price: $27.50
Market Value: $48

28

Sleighride
Issued: 1986 • Retired: 1990
#6511-0 • Orig. Price: $19.50
Market Value: $60

29
New

Tapping The Maples (set/7)
Issued: 1997 • Current
#56599 • Orig. Price: $75
Market Value: $75

30

Town Tinker (set/2)
Issued: 1992 • Retired: 1995
#5646-4 • Orig. Price: $24
Market Value: $35

31

Village Harvest People (set/4)
Issued: 1988 • Retired: 1991
#5941-2 • Orig. Price: $27.50
Market Value: $53

32

Woodcutter And Son (set/2)
Issued: 1988 • Retired: 1990
#5986-2 • Orig. Price: $10
Market Value: $53

NEW ENGLAND/ALPINE ACCESSORIES

Alpine Village

FACT FILE
Number of Accessories: 11
Year of First Issue: 1986
Current: 8
Retired: 3
Most Valuable: "Alpine Villagers" (set/3, $36)
New for 1998: 1

1

"Alpen Horn Player" Alpine Village Sign
Issued: 1995 • Current
#56182 • Orig. Price: $20
Market Value: $20

2

Alpine Village Sign
Issued: 1987 • Retired: 1993
#6571-4 • Orig. Price: $6
Market Value: $20

NEW ENGLAND VILLAGE

	Year Purch.	Price Paid	Value of My Collection
27.			
28.			
29.			
30.			
31.			
32.			

ALPINE VILLAGE

1.		
2.		

✎ PENCIL TOTALS

3

Alpine Villagers (set/3)
Issued: 1986 • Retired: 1992
#6542-0 • Orig. Price: $13
Market Value: $36

4

**Buying Bakers Bread
(set/2)**
Issued: 1992 • Retired: 1995
#5619-7 • Orig. Price: $20
Market Value: $35

5

**Climb Every Mountain
(set/4)**
Issued: 1993 • Current
#5613-8 • Orig. Price: $27.50
Market Value: $27.50

6
New

Heidi & Her Goats (set/4)
Issued: 1997 • Current
#56201 • Orig. Price: $30
Market Value: $30

7

**A New Batch Of
Christmas Friends (set/3)**
Issued: 1997 • Current
#56175 • Orig. Price: $27.50
Market Value: $27.50

8

**Nutcracker Vendor
& Cart**
Issued: 1996 • Current
#56183 • Orig. Price: $25
Market Value: $25

Alpine Village

	Year Purch.	Price Paid	Value of My Collection
3.			
4.			
5.			
6.			
7.			
8.			
9.			
10.			
11.			

PENCIL TOTALS

9

Polka Fest (set/3)
Issued: 1994 • Current
#5607-3 • Orig. Price: $30
Market Value: $30

10

"Silent Night" Music Box
Issued: 1995 • Current
#56180 • Orig. Price: $32.50
Market Value: $32.50

11

The Toy Peddler (set/3)
Issued: 1990 • Current
#5616-2 • Orig. Price: $22
Market Value: $22

Christmas in the City

FACT FILE
Number of Accessories: 41
Year of First Issue: 1987
Current: 20
Retired: 21
Most Valuable: "Salvation Army Band" (set/6, $94)
New for 1998: 6

CHRISTMAS IN THE CITY

①

All Around The Town (set/2)
Issued: 1991 • Retired: 1993
#5545-0 • Orig. Price: $18
Market Value: $32

②

Automobiles (set/3)
Issued: 1987 • Retired: 1996
#5964-1 • Orig. Price: $15
Market Value: $28

③
New

Big Smile For The Camera (set/2)
Issued: 1997 • Current
#58900 • Orig. Price: $27.50
Market Value: $27.50

④

Boulevard (set/14)
Issued: 1989 • Retired: 1992
#5516-6 • Orig. Price: $25
Market Value: $62

⑤

Busy Sidewalks (set/4)
Issued: 1990 • Retired: 1992
#5535-2 • Orig. Price: $28
Market Value: $50

⑥

Caroling Thru The City (set/3)
Issued: 1991 • Current
#5548-4 • Orig. Price: $27.50
Market Value: $27.50

⑦

Central Park Carriage
Issued: 1989 • Current
#5979-0 • Orig. Price: $30
Market Value: $30

⑧

Chamber Orchestra (set/4)
Issued: 1994 • Current
#5884-0 • Orig. Price: $37.50
Market Value: $37.50

CHRISTMAS IN THE CITY

	Year Purch.	Price Paid	Value of My Collection
1.			
2.			
3.			
4.			
5.			
6.			
7.			
8.			
		PENCIL TOTALS	

CHRISTMAS IN THE CITY
ACCESSORIES

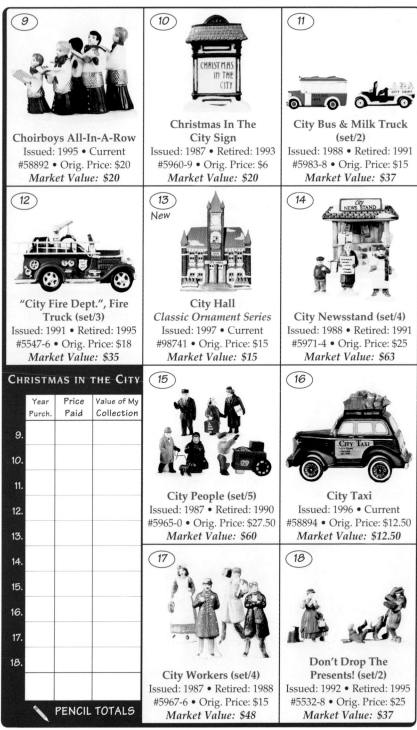

9

Choirboys All-In-A-Row
Issued: 1995 • Current
#58892 • Orig. Price: $20
Market Value: $20

10

**Christmas In The
City Sign**
Issued: 1987 • Retired: 1993
#5960-9 • Orig. Price: $6
Market Value: $20

11

**City Bus & Milk Truck
(set/2)**
Issued: 1988 • Retired: 1991
#5983-8 • Orig. Price: $15
Market Value: $37

12

**"City Fire Dept.", Fire
Truck (set/3)**
Issued: 1991 • Retired: 1995
#5547-6 • Orig. Price: $18
Market Value: $35

13
New

City Hall
Classic Ornament Series
Issued: 1997 • Current
#98741 • Orig. Price: $15
Market Value: $15

14

City Newsstand (set/4)
Issued: 1988 • Retired: 1991
#5971-4 • Orig. Price: $25
Market Value: $63

CHRISTMAS IN THE CITY

	Year Purch.	Price Paid	Value of My Collection
9.			
10.			
11.			
12.			
13.			
14.			
15.			
16.			
17.			
18.			

PENCIL TOTALS

15

City People (set/5)
Issued: 1987 • Retired: 1990
#5965-0 • Orig. Price: $27.50
Market Value: $60

16

City Taxi
Issued: 1996 • Current
#58894 • Orig. Price: $12.50
Market Value: $12.50

17

City Workers (set/4)
Issued: 1987 • Retired: 1988
#5967-6 • Orig. Price: $15
Market Value: $48

18

**Don't Drop The
Presents! (set/2)**
Issued: 1992 • Retired: 1995
#5532-8 • Orig. Price: $25
Market Value: $37

VALUE GUIDE — HERITAGE VILLAGE ACCESSORIES

(19) New

Dorothy's Dress Shop
Classic Ornament Series
Issued: 1997 • Current
#98740 • Orig. Price: $15
Market Value: $15

(20)

The Family Tree
Issued: 1996 • Current
#58895 • Orig. Price: $18
Market Value: $18

(21)

The Fire Brigade (set/2)
Issued: 1991 • Retired: 1995
#5546-8 • Orig. Price: $20
Market Value: $35

(22)

**Going Home For The
Holidays (set/3)**
Issued: 1996 • Current
#58896 • Orig. Price: $27.50
Market Value: $27.50

(23)

Holiday Field Trip (set/3)
Issued: 1994 • Current
#5885-8 • Orig. Price: $27.50
Market Value: $27.50

(24)

Hot Dog Vendor (set/3)
Issued: 1994 • Retired: 1997
#5886-6 • Orig. Price: $27.50
Market Value: $30

(25) New

**Johnson's Grocery . . .
Holiday Deliveries
(track compatible)**
Issued: 1997 • Current
#58897 • Orig. Price: $18
Market Value: $18

(26)

**"A Key To The City"
Christmas In The City Sign**
Issued: 1995 • Current
#58893 • Orig. Price: $20
Market Value: $20

(27) New

**Let's Go Shopping In
The City (set/3)**
Issued: 1997 • Current
#58899 • Orig. Price: $35
Market Value: $35

(28)

**Mailbox & Fire Hydrant
(set/2)**
Issued: 1989 • Retired: 1990
#5517-4 • Orig. Price: $6
Market Value: $25

CHRISTMAS IN THE CITY

	Year Purch.	Price Paid	Value of My Collection
19.			
20.			
21.			
22.			
23.			
24.			
25.			
26.			
27.			
28.			
		✏ PENCIL TOTALS	

VALUE GUIDE — HERITAGE VILLAGE ACCESSORIES

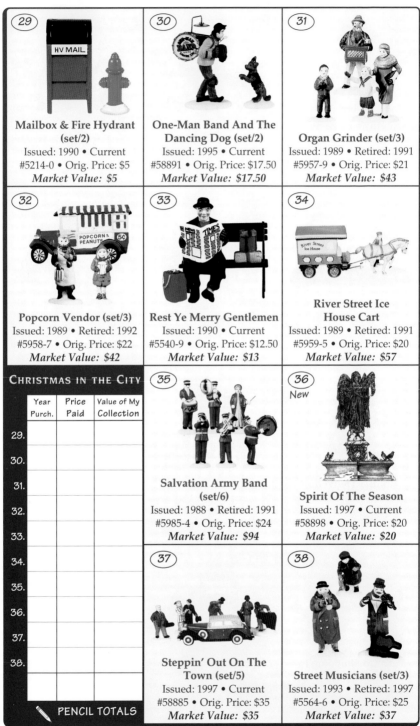

(29)

Mailbox & Fire Hydrant (set/2)
Issued: 1990 • Current
#5214-0 • Orig. Price: $5
Market Value: $5

(30)

One-Man Band And The Dancing Dog (set/2)
Issued: 1995 • Current
#58891 • Orig. Price: $17.50
Market Value: $17.50

(31)

Organ Grinder (set/3)
Issued: 1989 • Retired: 1991
#5957-9 • Orig. Price: $21
Market Value: $43

(32)

Popcorn Vendor (set/3)
Issued: 1989 • Retired: 1992
#5958-7 • Orig. Price: $22
Market Value: $42

(33)

Rest Ye Merry Gentlemen
Issued: 1990 • Current
#5540-9 • Orig. Price: $12.50
Market Value: $13

(34)

River Street Ice House Cart
Issued: 1989 • Retired: 1991
#5959-5 • Orig. Price: $20
Market Value: $57

CHRISTMAS IN THE CITY

	Year Purch.	Price Paid	Value of My Collection
29.			
30.			
31.			
32.			
33.			
34.			
35.			
36.			
37.			
38.			
PENCIL TOTALS			

(35)

Salvation Army Band (set/6)
Issued: 1988 • Retired: 1991
#5985-4 • Orig. Price: $24
Market Value: $94

(36) New

Spirit Of The Season
Issued: 1997 • Current
#58898 • Orig. Price: $20
Market Value: $20

(37)

Steppin' Out On The Town (set/5)
Issued: 1997 • Current
#58885 • Orig. Price: $35
Market Value: $35

(38)

Street Musicians (set/3)
Issued: 1993 • Retired: 1997
#5564-6 • Orig. Price: $25
Market Value: $37

'Tis The Season
Issued: 1990 • Retired: 1994
#5539-5 • Orig. Price: $12.50
Market Value: $26

Welcome Home (set/3)
Issued: 1992 • Retired: 1995
#5533-6 • Orig. Price: $27.50
Market Value: $42

"Yes, Virginia . . . " (set/2)
Issued: 1995 • Current
#58890 • Orig. Price: $12.50
Market Value: $12.50

North Pole

FACT FILE
Number of Accessories: 27
Year of First Issue: 1990
Current: 19
Retired: 8
**Most Valuable: "Letters
For Santa" (set/3, $65)**
New for 1998: 4

Baker Elves (set/3)
Issued: 1991 • Retired: 1995
#5603-0 • Orig. Price: $27.50
Market Value: $46

**"A Busy Elf"
North Pole Sign**
Issued: 1995 • Current
#56366 • Orig. Price: $20
Market Value: $20

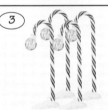

**Candy Cane
Lampposts (set/4)**
Issued: 1996 • Current
#52621 • Orig. Price: $13
Market Value: $12.50

**Charting Santa's
Course (set/2)**
Issued: 1995 • Retired: 1997
#56364 • Orig. Price: $25
Market Value: $32

New

**Delivering The Christmas
Greens (set/2)**
Issued: 1997 • Current
#56373 • Orig. Price: $27.50
Market Value: $27.50

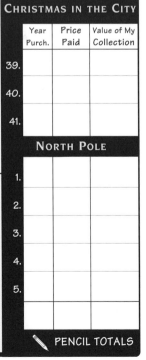

CHRISTMAS IN THE CITY

	Year Purch.	Price Paid	Value of My Collection
39.			
40.			
41.			

NORTH POLE

1.			
2.			
3.			
4.			
5.			

✎ **PENCIL TOTALS**

CHRISTMAS/NORTH POLE ACCESSORIES

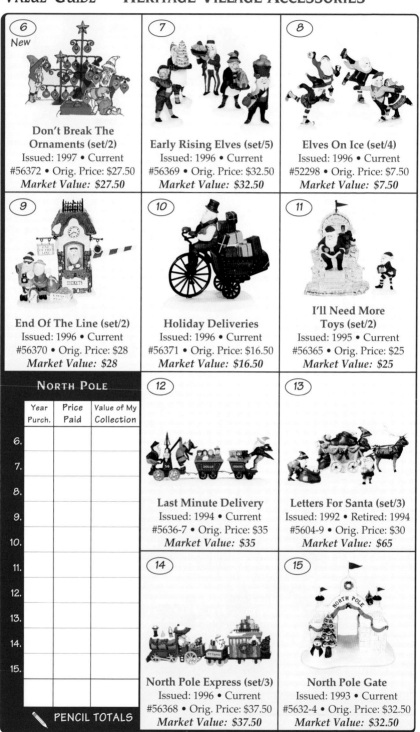

6
New

Don't Break The Ornaments (set/2)
Issued: 1997 • Current
#56372 • Orig. Price: $27.50
Market Value: $27.50

7

Early Rising Elves (set/5)
Issued: 1996 • Current
#56369 • Orig. Price: $32.50
Market Value: $32.50

8

Elves On Ice (set/4)
Issued: 1996 • Current
#52298 • Orig. Price: $7.50
Market Value: $7.50

9

End Of The Line (set/2)
Issued: 1996 • Current
#56370 • Orig. Price: $28
Market Value: $28

10

Holiday Deliveries
Issued: 1996 • Current
#56371 • Orig. Price: $16.50
Market Value: $16.50

11

I'll Need More Toys (set/2)
Issued: 1995 • Current
#56365 • Orig. Price: $25
Market Value: $25

North Pole

	Year Purch.	Price Paid	Value of My Collection
6.			
7.			
8.			
9.			
10.			
11.			
12.			
13.			
14.			
15.			

✏ PENCIL TOTALS

12

Last Minute Delivery
Issued: 1994 • Current
#5636-7 • Orig. Price: $35
Market Value: $35

13

Letters For Santa (set/3)
Issued: 1992 • Retired: 1994
#5604-9 • Orig. Price: $30
Market Value: $65

14

North Pole Express (set/3)
Issued: 1996 • Current
#56368 • Orig. Price: $37.50
Market Value: $37.50

15

North Pole Gate
Issued: 1993 • Current
#5632-4 • Orig. Price: $32.50
Market Value: $32.50

16

North Pole Santa's Workshop
Classic Ornament Series
Issued: 1997 • Current
#98734 • Orig. Price: $16.50
Market Value: $16.50

17

Santa & Mrs. Claus (set/2)
Issued: 1990 • Current
#5609-0 • Orig. Price: $15
Market Value: $15

18

Santa's Little Helpers (set/3)
Issued: 1990 • Retired: 1993
#5610-3 • Orig. Price: $28
Market Value: $60

19
New

Santa's Lookout Tower
Classic Ornament Series
Issued: 1997 • Current
#98742 • Orig. Price: $15
Market Value: $15

20

Sing A Song For Santa (set/3)
Issued: 1993 • Current
#5631-6 • Orig. Price: $28
Market Value: $28

21

Sleigh & Eight Tiny Reindeer (set/5)
Issued: 1990 • Current
#5611-1 • Orig. Price: $40
Market Value: $42

22

Snow Cone Elves (set/4)
Issued: 1994 • Retired: 1997
#5637-5 • Orig. Price: $30
Market Value: $35

23

Testing The Toys (set/2)
Issued: 1992 • Current
#5605-7 • Orig. Price: $16.50
Market Value: $16.50

24

Toymaker Elves (set/3)
Issued: 1991 • Retired: 1995
#5602-2 • Orig. Price: $27.50
Market Value: $46

NORTH POLE ACCESSORIES

NORTH POLE

	Year Purch.	Price Paid	Value of My Collection
16.			
17.			
18.			
19.			
20.			
21.			
22.			
23.			
24.			

✏ PENCIL TOTALS

25

Trimming The North Pole
Issued: 1990 • Retired: 1993
#5608-1 • Orig. Price: $10
Market Value: $34

26
New

Untangle The Christmas Lights
Issued: 1997 • Current
#56374 • Orig. Price: $35
Market Value: $35

27

Woodsmen Elves (set/3)
Issued: 1993 • Retired: 1995
#5630-8 • Orig. Price: $30
Market Value: $53

Disney Parks Village Series

1

FACT FILE
Number of Accessories: 4
Year of First Issue: 1994
Current: 0
Retired: 4
Most Valuable: "Balloon Seller" (set/2, $60)
New for 1998: 0

Balloon Seller (set/2)
Issued: 1995 • Retired: 1996
#53539 • Orig. Price: $25
Market Value: $60

NORTH POLE

	Year Purch.	Price Paid	Value of My Collection
25.			
26.			
27.			

DISNEY PARKS VILLAGE SERIES

1.			
2.			
3.			
4.			

✏ PENCIL TOTALS

2

Disney Parks Family (set/3)
Issued: 1994 • Retired: 1996
#5354-6 • Orig. Price: $32.50
Market Value: $38

3

Mickey & Minnie (set/2)
Issued: 1994 • Retired: 1996
#5353-8 • Orig. Price: $22.50
Market Value: $31

4

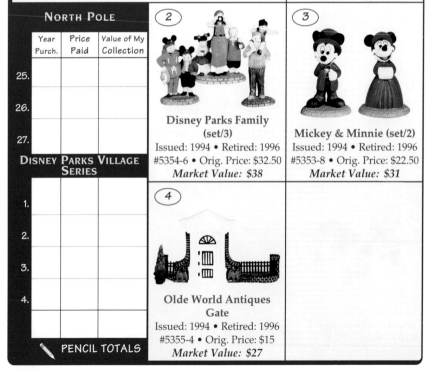

Olde World Antiques Gate
Issued: 1994 • Retired: 1996
#5355-4 • Orig. Price: $15
Market Value: $27

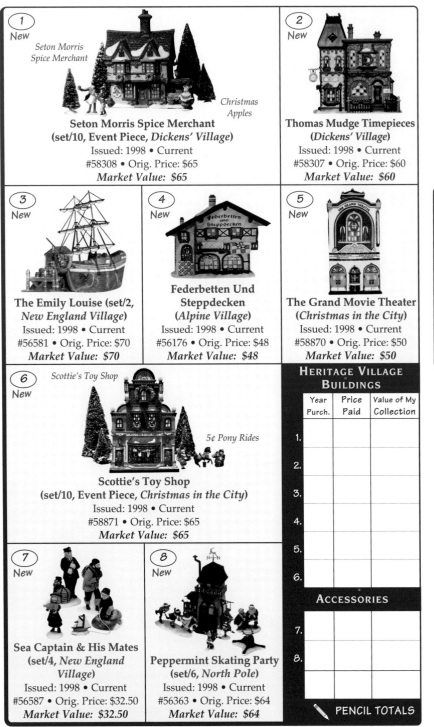

1
New

*Seton Morris
Spice Merchant*

*Christmas
Apples*

**Seton Morris Spice Merchant
(set/10, Event Piece, *Dickens' Village*)**
Issued: 1998 • Current
#58308 • Orig. Price: $65
Market Value: $65

2
New

Thomas Mudge Timepieces
(*Dickens' Village*)
Issued: 1998 • Current
#58307 • Orig. Price: $60
Market Value: $60

3
New

**The Emily Louise (set/2,
New England Village)**
Issued: 1998 • Current
#56581 • Orig. Price: $70
Market Value: $70

4
New

**Federbetten Und
Steppdecken
(*Alpine Village*)**
Issued: 1998 • Current
#56176 • Orig. Price: $48
Market Value: $48

5
New

The Grand Movie Theater
(*Christmas in the City*)
Issued: 1998 • Current
#58870 • Orig. Price: $50
Market Value: $50

6
New

Scottie's Toy Shop

5¢ Pony Rides

**Scottie's Toy Shop
(set/10, Event Piece, *Christmas in the City*)**
Issued: 1998 • Current
#58871 • Orig. Price: $65
Market Value: $65

7
New

**Sea Captain & His Mates
(set/4, *New England
Village*)**
Issued: 1998 • Current
#56587 • Orig. Price: $32.50
Market Value: $32.50

8
New

**Peppermint Skating Party
(set/6, *North Pole*)**
Issued: 1998 • Current
#56363 • Orig. Price: $64
Market Value: $64

**Heritage Village
Buildings**

	Year Purch.	Price Paid	Value of My Collection
1.			
2.			
3.			
4.			
5.			
6.			

Accessories

7.			
8.			

✏ **PENCIL TOTALS**

Mid-Year Releases

*Ask your local retailer or check our website (www.collectorspub.com) for information on a special
Department 56 lighted piece to be announced in late June.*

TOTAL VALUE OF MY COLLECTION

Record the value of your collection here by adding the pencil totals from the bottom of each value guide page.

HERITAGE VILLAGE BUILDINGS		
Page Number	Price Paid	Market Value
Page 31		
Page 32		
Page 33		
Page 34		
Page 35		
Page 36		
Page 37		
Page 38		
Page 39		
Page 40		
Page 41		
Page 42		
Page 43		
Page 44		
Page 45		
Page 46		
Page 47		
Page 48		
Page 49		
Page 50		
Page 51		
Page 52		
Page 53		
Page 54		
TOTAL		

HERITAGE VILLAGE BUILDINGS		
Page Number	Price Paid	Market Value
Page 55		
Page 56		
Page 57		
Page 58		
Page 59		
Page 60		
Page 61		
Page 62		
Page 63		
Page 64		
Page 65		
Page 66		
Page 67		
Page 68		
Page 69		
Page 70		
Page 71		
Page 72		
Page 73		
Page 74		
Page 75		
Page 76		
Page 105		
TOTAL		

TOTAL VALUE OF MY COLLECTION

HERITAGE VILLAGE ACCESSORIES		
Page Number	Price Paid	Market Value
Page 78		
Page 79		
Page 80		
Page 81		
Page 82		
Page 83		
Page 84		
Page 85		
Page 86		
Page 87		
Page 88		
Page 89		
Page 90		
Page 91		
TOTAL		

HERITAGE VILLAGE ACCESSORIES		
Page Number	Price Paid	Market Value
Page 92		
Page 93		
Page 94		
Page 95		
Page 96		
Page 97		
Page 98		
Page 99		
Page 100		
Page 101		
Page 102		
Page 103		
Page 104		
Page 105		
TOTAL		

GRAND TOTALS	
PRICE PAID	MARKET VALUE

HERITAGE VILLAGE TRIVIA QUIZ ANSWERS (FROM PAGE 77)

1. Queen Victoria 2. "The Nutcracker" 3. During a performance of "Henry VIII," a cannon was shot on stage causing the thatched roof to catch fire and the theater to burn to the ground. 4. *Dickens' Village* – "Chadbury Station And Train" and "Victoria Station," *New England Village* – "Weston Train Station," *Alpine Village* – "Bahnhof," *Christmas in the City* – "Grand Central Railway Station," *North Pole* – "North Pole Express Depot" 5. "St. Nikolaus Kirche" 6. N-O-R-T-H-P-O-L-E ("Neenee's Dolls & Toys," "Orly's Bell & Harness Supply," "Rimpy's Bakery," "Tassy's Mittens & Hassel's Woolies," "Post Office," "Obbie's Books & Letrinka's Candy," "Elfie's Sleds & Skates" 7. A foxhunt 8. "Cape Keag Fish Cannery" 9. Wackford Squeers 10. A costermonger was a peddler that sold goods from a pushcart

107

*S*ix brightly lit buildings debuted as Snow Village in 1976 and served as the catalyst for the creation of a whole new "cottage" industry. The Original Snow Village by Department 56 has grown by leaps and bounds to include 215 lighted buildings and 161 accessories. If in the beginning the village was considered a snapshot of a small village, it has since developed into a motion picture!

If you love Americana, you will love this village. Snow Village was originally set in the 1930s and 1940s, and captures the flavor of life in a typical small town. Some of the first pieces included "General Store" in 1978 and "Countryside Church" in 1979. These pieces were simpler, much like the era they're from. "The Christmas Shop" in 1991 and "Peppermint Porch Day Care" in 1995 may be more sophisticated in style and may come from a later era, but they still fit in nicely with the Snow Village theme and its new, expanded time line.

All kinds of businesses have opened their doors to the Snow Village community. Whether you are looking for a costume, a bouquet of flowers or a bagful of groceries, Snow Village can accommodate your needs! If

you have your eye on that "Nantucket Renovation" that's for sale, you could go to the "Village Realty" for more information, or if you're looking for something to zip around town on, you might like to check out the "Harley-Davidson® Motorcycle Shop."

Twenty years ago you may have had to leave town when looking for something to do, but this is certainly not a problem today, as there are many activities from which to choose. Like to bowl? Check out "Village Lanes." Bowling's not your bag? Like something with a bit more excitement? How about testing out the new skis you bought at the "Skate & Ski Shop." If you're not feeling that ambitious you can go antiquing at the local shops and perhaps at a couple of the barns on the outskirts of town. Wander on over to the village library, settle down into an overstuffed easy chair and catch up on the news.

Unlike Heritage Village, Snow Village does not have any clearly defined villages within it. However, Snow Village did issue the first of the *American Architecture Series* with "Queen Anne Victorian" and "Prairie House" in 1990. The series consists of nine homes built with distinctive American flair, including this year's release, "Italianate Villa."

In the early 1990s, Department 56 began to enter into licensing agreements with manufacturers and has since released buildings with recognizable names. In addition to the motorcycle shop, other brands now included are: Coca-Cola® with pieces like "Coca-Cola® Brand Bottling Plant," which came out in 1994 and Starbucks® Coffee with "Starbucks® Coffee," which was released in 1995. This year's releases include a "McDonald's®" that looks like it came right out of the early fifties, and a chocolate shop called "Hershey's™ Chocolate Shop."

With so many creative designs to choose from, Snow Village collectors can have a field day with all the display possibilities, from a charming residential neighborhood to a bustling downtown. Oh, what fun!

*A*t the beginning of 1998, nine new buildings and 16 new accessories were announced by Department 56 for The Original Snow Village.

The Brandon Bungalow . . . Named for a small Minnesota resort town, "The Brandon Bungalow" is one of several new private residences in Snow Village and features a front porch complete with white railing and stone support columns. The large second floor could be a spacious attic, or perhaps just a romper room for the kids. Of course, what family home would be complete without a shiny red car tucked inside the garage?

Christmas Barn Dance . . . A big sign advertising the "Christmas Barn Dance" hangs outside, drawing kids and adults from all over town. And when the crowd really gets going, the foot stompin' and fiddlin' echo all the way up the silo! Even if you don't two-step or square dance, you'll still enjoy this festive barn, which is decked out for the holidays with wreaths on the second-floor windows and a big Christmas tree out front.

Farm House . . . A new home graces the woodlands of Snow Village with the introduction of "Farm House." While several farmhouses have been introduced over the years, few have been as stately as this one, whose brick body and smooth tiled roof add a grand touch to the countryside. Elegant features of the "Farm House" include the porch's ornate border, white shutters that frame the first- and second-story windows and a large bay window featuring cheerful wax stenciling.

Gracie's Dry Goods & General Store (set/2) ... With its friendly service and wide selection of goods, "Gracie's Dry Goods & General Store" (set/2) is one of the most popular stops in town! Gracie made sure her store was easy to spot, thanks to its red front door, green bait shop on the side and a bright white second floor. Inside, the store has a little something for every villager who stops in. Motorists can even fill up their tanks at the pumping station outside (with the cheapest gas in town, of course).

Hershey's™ Chocolate Shop ... Everyone's talking about the new "Hershey's™ Chocolate Shop," a legendary (and sweet) piece of Americana that Snow Village collectors can now call their very own. And it's hard not to talk about the building: it has bright, fun colors and features a rooftop billboard illuminated by spotlights that highlight some of Hershey's most popular chocolates. Smaller billboards on the front of the building feature vintage images from Hershey's long history.

Italianate Villa ... The ninth piece in the *American Architecture Series* takes its name from the Italianate style, which is most commonly found in the northeastern United States. This elaborate two-story building exhibits many distinctive features: including tall, slender windows, a cupola, ornate bracketed cornices and a projecting porch, which also features a porch swing for those romantic evenings.

Linden Hills Country Club (set/2) . . . Finally, the Snow Village jet set have found a second home! Everything about the "Linden Hills Country Club" (set/2) speaks of class; from the building's brick construction and decorative iron grillwork, to the ornate "Linden Hills" signage. In addition to fine dining and a full bar, the country club features a pro shop where club members can replenish their supply of golf balls or order a set of custom-made clubs.

McDonald's® . . . Everyone's favorite restaurant has opened in Snow Village, bringing fun and food to adults and kids alike. It's a trip back in time with this beloved American symbol, as the piece features the classic design of the 1950s and offers hamburgers for only 15 cents! Unique features of "McDonald's®" include golden arches that really light up and kids sitting on the bench outside.

Rollerama Roller Rink . . . Snow Village has a new weekend hot spot! The "Rollerama Roller Rink" is a tip of the cap to the golden age of roller skating, a signature pastime for children of the 1950s and beyond. The building is bright and attractive and is illuminated by alternating red and green lights, while the yellow skylight on the roof really lights up.

Next to the entrance of the rink is a silhouette of a couple gracefully roller skating the night away, although the scene inside probably isn't so graceful!

Snow Village Accessories . . . One of the livelier new accessories, "At The Barn Dance, It's Allemande Left" (set/2), features holiday dancers flitting at the annual Christmas shindig. Another kind of excitement comes

from "Christmas Kids" (set/5), who march about toting gifts and wreaths for lucky recipients; while a young couple takes their poodle-skirted daughter out for a holiday skate in "Everybody Goes Skating At Rollerama" (set/2). A long-overdue accessory, "Farm Accessory Set" (set/35), offers everything collectors need for a complete farmyard scene in the largest accessory set ever released. A fun-loving snowman leads a group of kids in "He Led Them Down The Streets Of Town" (set/3); while in another part of the village, Santa himself has dropped in to oversee the making of a snowman replica of himself in "Santa Comes To Town, 1998," the fourth in an annul series of limited edition figurines.

Also new for 1998 are the "Village Animated Sledding Hill," as well as three accessories that can be used on the "Village Animated Accessory Track" that was issued in 1996: "Hitch-up The Buckboard," "A Holiday Sleigh Ride Together," and "Let It Snow, Let It Snow." Three delicious accessories that are perfect complements for the new Snow Village buildings are "Kids Love Hershey's™" (set/2), "Kids, Candy Canes . . . & Ronald McDonald®" (set/3) and "McDonald's® . . . Lights Up The Night." Three classic designs have been recast for the first Snow Village ornaments in the *Classic Ornament Series*: "J. Young's Granary," "Nantucket" and "Steepled

Dairy Barn

Federal House

Village Public Library

Mush!

Tour The Village

*D*epartment 56 announces Snow Village retirements each year and for the past several years the list has been published in *USA Today* as well as on the Department 56 website (*www.department56.com*). The following Snow Village pieces (listed with issue year in parentheses) were retired on November 6, 1997.

Snow Village Buildings
- ❏ All Saints Church (1986)
- ❏ Boulder Springs House (1996)
- ❏ Carmel Cottage (1994)
- ❏ Coca-Cola® Brand Bottling Plant (1994)
- ❏ Dairy Barn (1993)
- ❏ Federal House (1994)
  American Architecture Series
- ❏ Glenhaven House (1994)
- ❏ Gothic Farmhouse (1991)
  American Architecture Series
- ❏ Marvel's Beauty Salon (1994)
- ❏ Peppermint Porch Day Care (1995)
- ❏ Reindeer Bus Depot (1996)
- ❏ Ryman Auditorium® (1995)
- ❏ Village Public Library (1993)
- ❏ Village Station (1992)

Snow Village Accessories
- ❏ Coca-Cola® Brand Billboard (1994)
- ❏ Feeding The Birds (1994, set/3)
- ❏ Frosty Playtime (1995, set/3)
- ❏ Grand Ole Opry Carolers (1995)
- ❏ A Herd Of Holiday Heifers (1993, set/3)
- ❏ Mush! (1994, set/2)
- ❏ A Ride On The Reindeer Lines (1996, set/3)
- ❏ Safety Patrol (1993, set/4)
- ❏ Santa Comes To Town, 1997 (LE-1997)
- ❏ Tour The Village (1993)
- ❏ Village Used Car Lot (1992, set/5)

This section highlights the ten most valuable pieces in The Original Snow Village as determined by their value on the secondary market. In order to qualify for the Top Ten the pieces must have top dollar value and show a significant percentage increase from their original price, as shown by our Market Meter. Short production runs, breakage and purchases by people who were not collectors have all limited the available pool of each of these pieces.

 #1

ADOBE HOUSE
#5066-6
Issued 1979 — Retired 1980
Issue Price: $18
Secondary Market Price: $2,650
Market Meter: +14,622%

"Adobe House" entered the marketplace before the southwestern flair became evident in home decorating! Introduced in 1979, this unassuming adobe house did not receive a warm reception from Snow Village collectors, and was retired after only one year. Twenty years later, this piece is one of two that commands more than $2,000 on the secondary market!

#2

CATHEDRAL CHURCH
#5067-4
Issued 1980 — Retired 1981
Issue Price: $36
Secondary Market Price: $2,600
Market Meter: +7,122%

Snow Village collectors love churches and it's easy to understand why this church has made it to the #2 position. One of four churches in the Top Ten, the magnificent "Cathedral Church" experienced difficulties in the production stage. The complex design led to problems, including the collapse of the dome in the firing stage. Retired after only one year, few pieces are in circulation.

#3

MOBILE HOME
#5063-3
Issued 1979 — Retired 1980
Issue Price: $18
Secondary Market Price: $1,990
Market Meter: +10,956%

With its silver Airstream-style design, the "Mobile Home" looks like it came right off the pages of a travelogue from the fifties! Unfortunately, not many collectors liked the "Mobile Home" when it was first released in 1979. Today, however, many of them are wishing that they had that "Mobile Home" to park in their village, as its early retirement has caused its secondary market value to skyrocket. One reason the "Mobile Home" may be hard to find is because of its crossover appeal to recreational vehicle owners who are not collectors.

#4

MISSION CHURCH
#5062-5
Issued 1979 — Retired 1980
Issue Price: $30
Secondary Market Price: $1,260
Market Meter: +4,100%

A companion piece to the "Adobe House" (the #1 piece on our Top Ten list), the "Mission Church" received a less than enthusiastic reception when it was introduced to the public in 1979. The piece was retired after only one year of production and today it is highly sought after by general collectors of Snow Village, as well as those specifically target churches for their collections.

#5

SKATING RINK/DUCK POND SET
#5015-3
Issued 1978 — Retired 1979
Issue Price: $16
Secondary Market Price: $1,000
Market Meter: +6,150%

The two ponds in the "Skating Rink/Duck Pond Set" were the first pieces to be introduced to Snow Village that were not buildings. Each piece featured a pond surrounded by snow banks and a large lighted tree. In many instances, problems occurred where the tree joined the base, resulting in breakage, so this set was retired after only one year. Department 56 released another pond four years later, with the tree/base dilemma solved by a sturdier, two-part mold.

#6

STONE CHURCH
#5059-1
Issued 1979 — Retired 1980
Issue Price: $32
Secondary Market Price: $970
Market Meter: +2,931%

There have been three stone churches released by Department 56 for Snow Village and this can be a source of much confusion for collectors, especially due to the similarities between the first two. Introduced in 1979, the bright yellow "Stone Church" (the second "Stone Church" release) was available for just one year. This version of the church is 8.5" tall, with six or more window holes above the door. By contrast, the first "Stone Church" (#5009-6), released in 1977, is either a light mint green or pale yellow, stands 10.5" tall, and has three window holes above the door. Finally, the last release, "New Stone Church," has a different design altogether.

#7

CONGREGATIONAL CHURCH
#5034-2
Issued 1984 — Retired 1985
Issue Price: $28
Secondary Market Price: $640
Market Meter: +2,186%

Churches have often had problems during construction – both in real life as well as in Department 56's Snow Village – and the 1984 release, "Congregational Church," was no exception. The slender steeple was known to break off in production or in shipping, so the church was retired after only one year. This was the first time that a specific denomination was mentioned in the name of a church, and as a result this piece attracted casual buyers, therefore lessening the number of pieces available to collectors.

#8

DINER
#5078-4
Issued 1986 — Retired 1987
Issue Price: $22
Secondary Market Price: $630
Market Meter: +2,764%

This Snow Village "Diner" is based on an eatery in the Minneapolis/St. Paul area, which made the piece popular with residents of the Twin Cities. Known to many collectors simply as "Mickey's" because of the building's sign, this bright yellow dining car is a replica of a 1950s style restaurant. "Diner" retired after one year, which accounts for its rising value on the secondary market.

#9

FIRE STATION
#5032-6
Issued 1983 — Retired 1984
Issue Price: $32
Secondary Market Price: $629
Market Meter: +1,866%

The "Fire Station" appealed to many, and not just collectors, as this piece surely found its way into the homes of many firefighters during the one year that it was available. The doors of the station are swung open, revealing a pert dalmatian sitting in the fire truck, ready to go. Retired in 1984, this is a highly sought after piece. A follow-up piece, "Fire Station No. 2," was introduced in 1987.

#10

BANK
#5024-5
Issued 1982 — Retired 1983
Issue Price: $32
Secondary Market Price: $625
Market Meter: +1,853%

If you have the "Bank" you can rest assured that you've made a solid investment in the future! The "Bank" closes up the Snow Village Top Ten, snagging the 10th position. Available for just one year, this pieces had crossover appeal similar to the "Fire Station," as the building was scooped up by many in the banking business as well as collectors, making it a difficult piece to find on the secondary market.

How To Use Your Value Guide

1. Locate your piece in the value guide. This section lists the entire collection of The Original Snow Village. Lighted buildings are listed first, followed by a separate section of accessories. Every building and accessory is listed alphabetically, making it easy to locate your pieces. A special section featuring other Department 56 collectibles immediately follows the Snow Village accessories. This section features *Meadowland*, *Bachman's Hometown Series*, Canadian Exclusives and other special pieces produced by Department 56. Handy alphabetical and numerical indexes can be found in the back of the book.

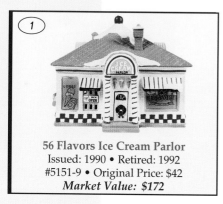

56 Flavors Ice Cream Parlor
Issued: 1990 • Retired: 1992
#5151-9 • Original Price: $42
Market Value: $172

2. Find the market value of your piece. Variations and their values are listed in parenthesis following the original piece's market value. Buildings or accessories for which secondary market pricing is not established are listed as "N/E."

3. Record the year you purchased the piece, the original price that you paid and the current value of the piece in the corresponding boxes at the bottom of the page.

4. Calculate the total value for the entire page by adding together all of the boxes in each column. Use a pencil so you can change the totals as your collection grows!

5. Transfer the totals from each page to the "Total Value Of My Collection" worksheet on page 174.

6. Add all of the totals together to determine the overall value of your collection.

SNOW VILLAGE		
Year Purchased	Price Paid	Value of My Collection
1.		
2.		
3.		
4.		
5.		
PENCIL TOTALS		

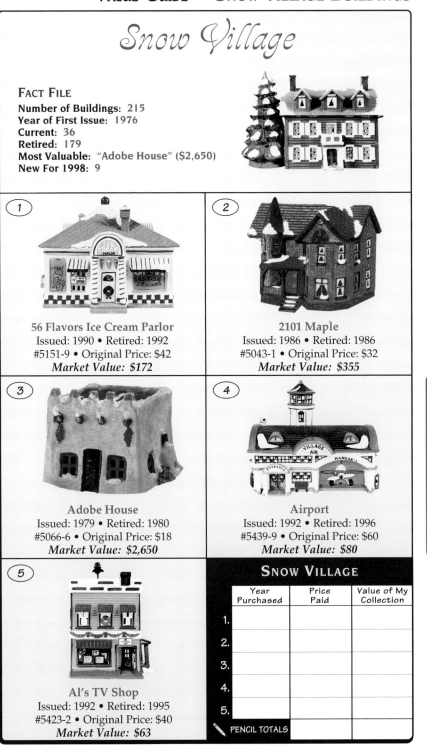

Snow Village

FACT FILE

Number of Buildings: 215
Year of First Issue: 1976
Current: 36
Retired: 179
Most Valuable: "Adobe House" ($2,650)
New For 1998: 9

1

56 Flavors Ice Cream Parlor
Issued: 1990 • Retired: 1992
#5151-9 • Original Price: $42
Market Value: $172

2

2101 Maple
Issued: 1986 • Retired: 1986
#5043-1 • Original Price: $32
Market Value: $355

3

Adobe House
Issued: 1979 • Retired: 1980
#5066-6 • Original Price: $18
Market Value: $2,650

4

Airport
Issued: 1992 • Retired: 1996
#5439-9 • Original Price: $60
Market Value: $80

5

Al's TV Shop
Issued: 1992 • Retired: 1995
#5423-2 • Original Price: $40
Market Value: $63

SNOW VILLAGE

	Year Purchased	Price Paid	Value of My Collection
1.			
2.			
3.			
4.			
5.			
PENCIL TOTALS			

SNOW VILLAGE BUILDINGS

6

All Saints Church
Issued: 1986 • Retired: 1997
#5070-9 • Original Price: $38
Market Value: $52

7

Apothecary
Issued: 1986 • Retired: 1990
#5076-8 • Original Price: $34
Market Value: $108

8

Bakery
Issued: 1981 • Retired: 1983
#5077-6 • Original Price: $30
Market Value: $285

9

Bakery
Issued: 1986 • Retired: 1991
#5077-6 • Original Price: $35
Market Value: $90

10

Bank
Issued: 1982 • Retired: 1983
#5024-5 • Original Price: $32
Market Value: $625

11

Barn
Issued: 1981 • Retired: 1984
#5074-1 • Original Price: $32
Market Value: $447

Snow Village

	Year Purchased	Price Paid	Value of My Collection
6.			
7.			
8.			
9.			
10.			
11.			
12.			
PENCIL TOTALS			

12

Bayport
Issued: 1984 • Retired: 1986
#5015-6 • Original Price: $30
Market Value: $240

13

Beacon Hill House
Issued: 1986 • Retired: 1988
#5065-2 • Original Price: $31
Market Value: $175

14

Beacon Hill Victorian
Issued: 1995 • Current
#54857 • Original Price: $60
Market Value: $60

15

Birch Run Ski Chalet
Issued: 1996 • Current
#54882 • Original Price: $60
Market Value: $60

16

Boulder Springs House
Issued: 1996 • Retired: 1997
#54873 • Original Price: $60
Market Value: $64

17

Bowling Alley
Issued: 1995 • Current
#54858 • Original Price: $42
Market Value: $42

18
New

The Brandon Bungalow
Issued: 1997 • Current
#54918 • Original Price: $55
Market Value: $55

19

Brownstone
Issued: 1979 • Retired: 1981
#5056-7 • Original Price: $36
Market Value: $570

SNOW VILLAGE

	Year Purchased	Price Paid	Value of My Collection
13.			
14.			
15.			
16.			
17.			
18.			
19.			
PENCIL TOTALS			

SNOW VILLAGE BUILDINGS

20

Cape Cod
Issued: 1978 • Retired: 1980
#5013-8 • Original Price: $20
Market Value: $394

21

Carmel Cottage
Issued: 1994 • Retired: 1997
#5466-6 • Original Price: $48
Market Value: $60

22

Carriage House
Issued: 1982 • Retired: 1984
#5021-0 • Original Price: $28
Market Value: $338

23

Carriage House
Issued: 1986 • Retired: 1988
#5071-7 • Original Price: $29
Market Value: $125

24

Cathedral Church
Issued: 1980 • Retired: 1981
#5067-4 • Original Price: $36
Market Value: $2,600

25

Cathedral Church
Issued: 1987 • Retired: 1990
#5019-9 • Original Price: $50
Market Value: $120

SNOW VILLAGE

	Year Purchased	Price Paid	Value of My Collection
20.			
21.			
22.			
23.			
24.			
25.			
26.			
✎ PENCIL TOTALS			

26

Centennial House
Issued: 1982 • Retired: 1984
#5020-2 • Original Price: $32
Market Value: $350

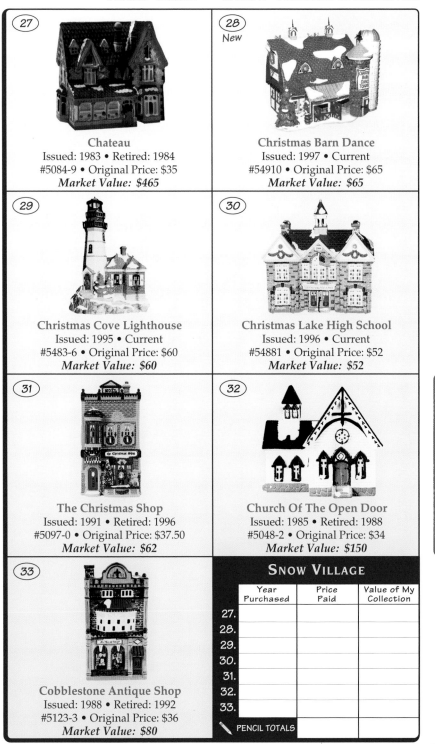

27

Chateau
Issued: 1983 • Retired: 1984
#5084-9 • Original Price: $35
Market Value: $465

28
New

Christmas Barn Dance
Issued: 1997 • Current
#54910 • Original Price: $65
Market Value: $65

29

Christmas Cove Lighthouse
Issued: 1995 • Current
#5483-6 • Original Price: $60
Market Value: $60

30

Christmas Lake High School
Issued: 1996 • Current
#54881 • Original Price: $52
Market Value: $52

31

The Christmas Shop
Issued: 1991 • Retired: 1996
#5097-0 • Original Price: $37.50
Market Value: $62

32

Church Of The Open Door
Issued: 1985 • Retired: 1988
#5048-2 • Original Price: $34
Market Value: $150

33

Cobblestone Antique Shop
Issued: 1988 • Retired: 1992
#5123-3 • Original Price: $36
Market Value: $80

SNOW VILLAGE

	Year Purchased	Price Paid	Value of My Collection
27.			
28.			
29.			
30.			
31.			
32.			
33.			
PENCIL TOTALS			

SNOW VILLAGE BUILDINGS

(34)

Coca-Cola® Brand Bottling Plant
Issued: 1994 • Retired: 1997
#5469-0 • Original Price: $65
Market Value: $78

(35)

Coca-Cola® Brand Corner Drugstore
Issued: 1995 • Current
#5484-4 • Original Price: $55
Market Value: $55

(36)

Colonial Church
Issued: 1989 • Retired: 1992
#5119-5 • Original Price: $60
Market Value: $80

(37)

Colonial Farm House
Issued: 1980 • Retired: 1982
#5070-9 • Original Price: $30
Market Value: $335

(38)

Congregational Church
Issued: 1984 • Retired: 1985
#5034-2 • Original Price: $28
Market Value: $640

(39)

Corner Cafe
Issued: 1988 • Retired: 1991
#5124-1 • Original Price: $37
Market Value: $98

Snow Village

	Year Purchased	Price Paid	Value of My Collection
34.			
35.			
36.			
37.			
38.			
39.			
40.			
✏ PENCIL TOTALS			

(40)

Corner Store
Issued: 1981 • Retired: 1983
#5076-8 • Original Price: $30
Market Value: $255

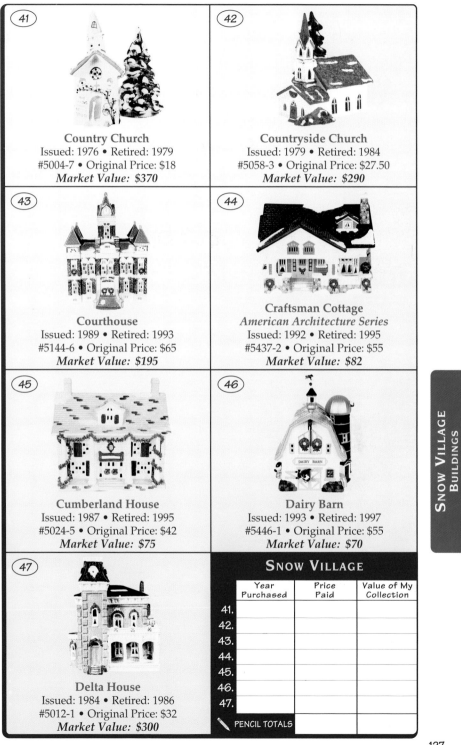

(41)

Country Church
Issued: 1976 • Retired: 1979
#5004-7 • Original Price: $18
Market Value: $370

(42)

Countryside Church
Issued: 1979 • Retired: 1984
#5058-3 • Original Price: $27.50
Market Value: $290

(43)

Courthouse
Issued: 1989 • Retired: 1993
#5144-6 • Original Price: $65
Market Value: $195

(44)

Craftsman Cottage
American Architecture Series
Issued: 1992 • Retired: 1995
#5437-2 • Original Price: $55
Market Value: $82

(45)

Cumberland House
Issued: 1987 • Retired: 1995
#5024-5 • Original Price: $42
Market Value: $75

(46)

Dairy Barn
Issued: 1993 • Retired: 1997
#5446-1 • Original Price: $55
Market Value: $70

(47)

Delta House
Issued: 1984 • Retired: 1986
#5012-1 • Original Price: $32
Market Value: $300

SNOW VILLAGE

	Year Purchased	Price Paid	Value of My Collection
41.			
42.			
43.			
44.			
45.			
46.			
47.			
PENCIL TOTALS			

SNOW VILLAGE BUILDINGS

(48)

**Depot & Train With
Two Train Cars (set/2)**
Issued: 1985 • Retired: 1988
#5051-2 • Original Price: $65
Market Value: $135

(49)

Dinah's Drive-In
Issued: 1993 • Retired: 1996
#5447-0 • Original Price: $45
Market Value: $80

(50)

Diner
Issued: 1986 • Retired: 1987
#5078-4 • Original Price: $22
Market Value: $630

(51)

Doctor's House
Issued: 1989 • Retired: 1992
#5143-8 • Original Price: $56
Market Value: $105

(52)

Double Bungalow
Issued: 1991 • Retired: 1994
#5407-0 • Original Price: $45
Market Value: $70

(53)

Duplex
Issued: 1985 • Retired: 1987
#5050-4 • Original Price: $35
Market Value: $172

SNOW VILLAGE

	Year Purchased	Price Paid	Value of My Collection
48.			
49.			
50.			
51.			
52.			
53.			
54.			
✏ PENCIL TOTALS			

(54)

Dutch Colonial
American Architecture Series
Issued: 1995 • Retired: 1996
#54856 • Original Price: $45
Market Value: $62

55

English Church
Issued: 1981 • Retired: 1982
#5078-4 • Original Price: $30
Market Value: $383

56

English Cottage
Issued: 1981 • Retired: 1982
#5073-3 • Original Price: $25
Market Value: $310

57

English Tudor
Issued: 1983 • Retired: 1985
#5033-4 • Original Price: $30
Market Value: $288

58

Farm House
Issued: 1987 • Retired: 1992
#5089-0 • Original Price: $40
Market Value: $77

59
New

Farm House
Issued: 1997 • Current
#54912 • Original Price: $50
Market Value: $50

60

Federal House
American Architecture Series
Issued: 1994 • Retired: 1997
#5465-8 • Original Price: $50
Market Value: $62

61

Finklea's Finery: Costume Shop
Issued: 1991 • Retired: 1993
#5405-4 • Original Price: $45
Market Value: $72

SNOW VILLAGE

	Year Purchased	Price Paid	Value of My Collection
55.			
56.			
57.			
58.			
59.			
60.			
61.			
✏ PENCIL TOTALS			

SNOW VILLAGE BUILDINGS

62

Fire Station
Issued: 1983 • Retired: 1984
#5032-6 • Original Price: $32
Market Value: $629

63

Fire Station No. 2
Issued: 1987 • Retired: 1989
#5091-1 • Original Price: $40
Market Value: $220

64

Trout   *Bass*
Fisherman's Nook Cabins (set/2)
Issued: 1994 • Current
#5461-5 • Original Price: $50
Market Value: $50

65

Fisherman's Nook Resort
Issued: 1994 • Current
#5460-7 • Original Price: $75
Market Value: $75

66

Flower Shop
Issued: 1982 • Retired: 1983
#5082-2 • Original Price: $25
Market Value: $468

67

Gabled Cottage
Issued: 1976 • Retired: 1979
#5002-1 • Original Price: $20
Market Value: $380

SNOW VILLAGE

	Year Purchased	Price Paid	Value of My Collection
62.			
63.			
64.			
65.			
66.			
67.			
PENCIL TOTALS			

68

Gabled House
Issued: 1982 • Retired: 1983
#5081-4 • Original Price: $30
Market Value: $425

69

Galena House
Issued: 1984 • Retired: 1985
#5009-1 • Original Price: $32
Market Value: $340

70

Version 2

Version 3

General Store
Issued: 1978 • Retired: 1980
#5012-0 • Original Price: $25
Market Value: $472 (tan – $610, gold – $545)

71

Giant Trees
Issued: 1979 • Retired: 1982
#5065-8 • Original Price: $20
Market Value: $340

72

Version 2

Gingerbread House (coin bank)
Issued: 1983 • Retired: 1984
#5025-3 • Original Price: $24
Market Value: $310 (lit house – $310)

73

Glenhaven House
Issued: 1994 • Retired: 1997
#5468-2 • Original Price: $45
Market Value: $60

SNOW VILLAGE

	Year Purchased	Price Paid	Value of My Collection
68.			
69.			
70.			
71.			
72.			
73.			
PENCIL TOTALS			

SNOW VILLAGE BUILDINGS

74

**Good Shepherd Chapel
& Church School (set/2)**
Issued: 1992 • Retired: 1996
#5424-0 • Original Price: $72
Market Value: $102

75

Gothic Church
Issued: 1983 • Retired: 1986
#5028-8 • Original Price: $36
Market Value: $270

76

Gothic Farmhouse
American Architecture Series
Issued: 1991 • Retired: 1997
#5404-6 • Original Price: $48
Market Value: $52

77

Governor's Mansion
Issued: 1983 • Retired: 1985
#5003-2 • Original Price: $32
Market Value: $315

78
New

**Gracie's Dry Goods
& General Store (set/2)**
Issued: 1997 • Current
#54915 • Original Price: $70
Market Value: $70

79

Grandma's Cottage
Issued: 1992 • Retired: 1996
#5420-8 • Original Price: $42
Market Value: $65

SNOW VILLAGE

	Year Purchased	Price Paid	Value of My Collection
74.			
75.			
76.			
77.			
78.			
79.			
80.			
PENCIL TOTALS			

80

Grocery
Issued: 1983 • Retired: 1985
#5001-6 • Original Price: $35
Market Value: $357

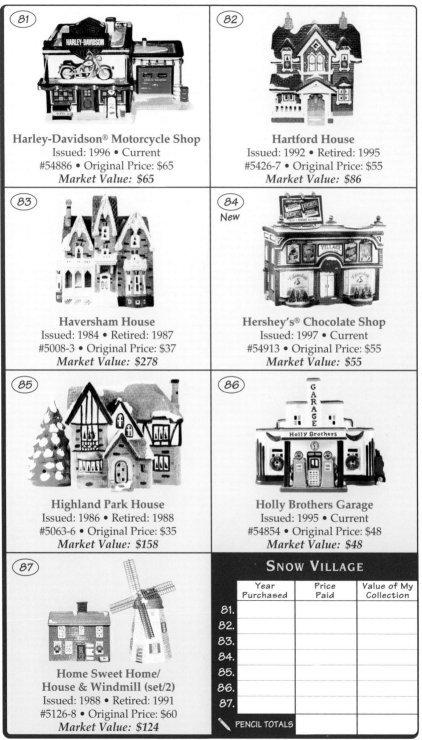

81

Harley-Davidson® Motorcycle Shop
Issued: 1996 • Current
#54886 • Original Price: $65
Market Value: $65

82

Hartford House
Issued: 1992 • Retired: 1995
#5426-7 • Original Price: $55
Market Value: $86

83

Haversham House
Issued: 1984 • Retired: 1987
#5008-3 • Original Price: $37
Market Value: $278

84 New

Hershey's® Chocolate Shop
Issued: 1997 • Current
#54913 • Original Price: $55
Market Value: $55

85

Highland Park House
Issued: 1986 • Retired: 1988
#5063-6 • Original Price: $35
Market Value: $158

86

Holly Brothers Garage
Issued: 1995 • Current
#54854 • Original Price: $48
Market Value: $48

87

Home Sweet Home/
House & Windmill (set/2)
Issued: 1988 • Retired: 1991
#5126-8 • Original Price: $60
Market Value: $124

SNOW VILLAGE BUILDINGS

SNOW VILLAGE

	Year Purchased	Price Paid	Value of My Collection
81.			
82.			
83.			
84.			
85.			
86.			
87.			
PENCIL TOTALS			

133

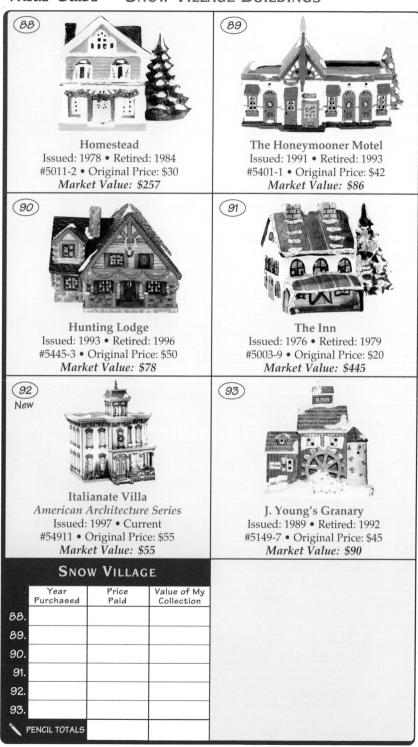

(88)

Homestead
Issued: 1978 • Retired: 1984
#5011-2 • Original Price: $30
Market Value: $257

(89)

The Honeymooner Motel
Issued: 1991 • Retired: 1993
#5401-1 • Original Price: $42
Market Value: $86

(90)

Hunting Lodge
Issued: 1993 • Retired: 1996
#5445-3 • Original Price: $50
Market Value: $78

(91)

The Inn
Issued: 1976 • Retired: 1979
#5003-9 • Original Price: $20
Market Value: $445

(92)
New

Italianate Villa
American Architecture Series
Issued: 1997 • Current
#54911 • Original Price: $55
Market Value: $55

(93)

J. Young's Granary
Issued: 1989 • Retired: 1992
#5149-7 • Original Price: $45
Market Value: $90

SNOW VILLAGE

	Year Purchased	Price Paid	Value of My Collection
88.			
89.			
90.			
91.			
92.			
93.			
PENCIL TOTALS			

94

Jack's Corner Barber Shop
Issued: 1991 • Retired: 1994
#5406-2 • Original Price: $42
Market Value: $72

95

Jefferson School
Issued: 1987 • Retired: 1991
#5082-2 • Original Price: $36
Market Value: $170

96

Jingle Belle Houseboat
Issued: 1989 • Retired: 1991
#5114-4 • Original Price: $42
Market Value: $162

97

Kenwood House
Issued: 1988 • Retired: 1990
#5054-7 • Original Price: $50
Market Value: $138

98

Version 2

Knob Hill
Issued: 1979 • Retired: 1981
#5055-9 • Original Price: $30
Market Value: $390 (yellow – $370)

99

Large Single Tree
Issued: 1981 • Retired: 1989
#5080-6 • Original Price: $17
Market Value: $50

Snow Village Buildings

Snow Village

	Year Purchased	Price Paid	Value of My Collection
94.			
95.			
96.			
97.			
98.			
99.			
PENCIL TOTALS			

100

Lighthouse
Issued: 1987 • Retired: 1988
#5030-0 • Original Price: $36
Market Value: $594

101

Lincoln Park Duplex
Issued: 1986 • Retired: 1988
#5060-1 • Original Price: $33
Market Value: $140

102

New

Linden Hills Country Club (set/2)
Issued: 1997 • Current
#54917 • Original Price: $60
Market Value: $60

103

Log Cabin
Issued: 1979 • Retired: 1981
#5057-5 • Original Price: $22
Market Value: $500

104

Main Street House
Issued: 1984 • Retired: 1986
#5005-9 • Original Price: $27
Market Value: $255

105

Mainstreet Gift Shop
(GCC Piece)
Issued: 1997 • Retired: 1997
#54887 • Original Price: $50
Market Value: N/E

Snow Village

	Year Purchased	Price Paid	Value of My Collection
100.			
101.			
102.			
103.			
104.			
105.			
106.			
PENCIL TOTALS			

106

Mainstreet Hardware Store
Issued: 1990 • Retired: 1993
#5153-5 • Original Price: $42
Market Value: $84

(107)

Mansion
Issued: 1977 • Retired: 1979
#5008-8 • Original Price: $30
Market Value: $500

(108)

Maple Ridge Inn
Issued: 1988 • Retired: 1990
#5121-7 • Original Price: $55
Market Value: $84

(109)

Marvel's Beauty Salon
Issued: 1994 • Retired: 1997
#5470-4 • Original Price: $37.50
Market Value: $50

(110)
New

McDonald's®
Issued: 1997 • Current
#54914 • Original Price: $65
Market Value: $65

(111)

Mission Church
Issued: 1979 • Retired: 1980
#5062-5 • Original Price: $30
Market Value: $1,260

(112)

Mobile Home
Issued: 1979 • Retired: 1980
#5063-3 • Original Price: $18
Market Value: $1,990

(113)

Morningside House
Issued: 1990 • Retired: 1992
#5152-7 • Original Price: $45
Market Value: $67

SNOW VILLAGE

	Year Purchased	Price Paid	Value of My Collection
107.			
108.			
109.			
110.			
111.			
112.			
113.			
✏ PENCIL TOTALS			

SNOW VILLAGE BUILDINGS

(114)

Mount Olivet Church
Issued: 1993 • Retired: 1996
#5442-9 • Original Price: $65
Market Value: $80

(115)

Mountain Lodge
Issued: 1976 • Retired: 1979
#5001-3 • Original Price: $20
Market Value: $378

(116)

Nantucket
Issued: 1978 • Retired: 1986
#5014-6 • Original Price: $25
Market Value: $265

(117)

Nantucket Renovation (LE-1993)
Issued: 1993 • Retired: 1993
#5441-0 • Original Price: $55
Market Value: $79

(118)

New Hope Church
Issued: 1997 • Current
#54904 • Original Price: $60
Market Value: $60

(119)

New School House
Issued: 1984 • Retired: 1986
#5037-7 • Original Price: $35
Market Value: $260

Snow Village

	Year Purchased	Price Paid	Value of My Collection
114.			
115.			
116.			
117.			
118.			
119.			
120.			
PENCIL TOTALS			

(120)

New Stone Church
Issued: 1982 • Retired: 1984
#5083-0 • Original Price: $32
Market Value: $387

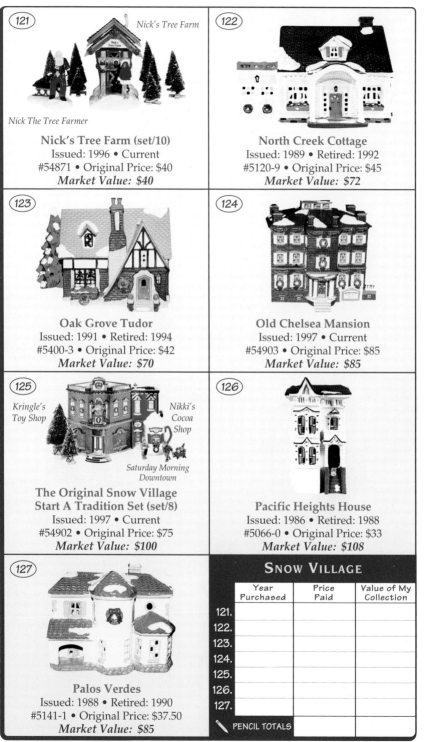

(121)

Nick's Tree Farm

Nick The Tree Farmer

Nick's Tree Farm (set/10)
Issued: 1996 • Current
#54871 • Original Price: $40
Market Value: $40

(122)

North Creek Cottage
Issued: 1989 • Retired: 1992
#5120-9 • Original Price: $45
Market Value: $72

(123)

Oak Grove Tudor
Issued: 1991 • Retired: 1994
#5400-3 • Original Price: $42
Market Value: $70

(124)

Old Chelsea Mansion
Issued: 1997 • Current
#54903 • Original Price: $85
Market Value: $85

(125)

Kringle's Toy Shop

Nikki's Cocoa Shop

Saturday Morning Downtown

The Original Snow Village Start A Tradition Set (set/8)
Issued: 1997 • Current
#54902 • Original Price: $75
Market Value: $100

(126)

Pacific Heights House
Issued: 1986 • Retired: 1988
#5066-0 • Original Price: $33
Market Value: $108

(127)

Palos Verdes
Issued: 1988 • Retired: 1990
#5141-1 • Original Price: $37.50
Market Value: $85

SNOW VILLAGE

	Year Purchased	Price Paid	Value of My Collection
121.			
122.			
123.			
124.			
125.			
126.			
127.			
PENCIL TOTALS			

SNOW VILLAGE BUILDINGS

(128)

Paramount Theater
Issued: 1989 • Retired: 1993
#5142-0 • Original Price: $42
Market Value: $170

(129)

Parish Church
Issued: 1984 • Retired: 1986
#5039-3 • Original Price: $32
Market Value: $322

(130)

Parsonage
Issued: 1983 • Retired: 1985
#5029-6 • Original Price: $35
Market Value: $370

(131)

Peppermint Porch Day Care
Issued: 1995 • Retired: 1997
#5485-2 • Original Price: $45
Market Value: $50

(132)

Pinewood Log Cabin
Issued: 1989 • Retired: 1995
#5150-0 • Original Price: $37.50
Market Value: $68

(133)

Pioneer Church
Issued: 1982 • Retired: 1984
#5022-9 • Original Price: $30
Market Value: $344

Snow Village

	Year Purchased	Price Paid	Value of My Collection
128.			
129.			
130.			
131.			
132.			
133.			
134.			
PENCIL TOTALS			

(134)

Pisa Pizza
Issued: 1995 • Current
#54851 • Original Price: $35
Market Value: $35

(135)

Plantation House
Issued: 1985 • Retired: 1987
#5047-4 • Original Price: $37
Market Value: $123

(136)

Prairie House
American Architecture Series
Issued: 1990 • Retired: 1993
#5156-0 • Original Price: $42
Market Value: $73

(137)

Print Shop & Village News
Issued: 1992 • Retired: 1994
#5425-9 • Original Price: $37.50
Market Value: $74

(138)

Queen Anne Victorian
American Architecture Series
Issued: 1990 • Retired: 1996
#5157-8 • Original Price: $48
Market Value: $70

(139)

Ramsey Hill House
Issued: 1986 • Retired: 1989
#5067-9 • Original Price: $36
Market Value: $100

(140)

Red Barn
Issued: 1987 • Retired: 1992
#5081-4 • Original Price: $38
Market Value: $92

(141)

Redeemer Church
Issued: 1988 • Retired: 1992
#5127-6 • Original Price: $42
Market Value: $71

SNOW VILLAGE BUILDINGS

SNOW VILLAGE

	Year Purchased	Price Paid	Value of My Collection
135.			
136.			
137.			
138.			
139.			
140.			
141.			
PENCIL TOTALS			

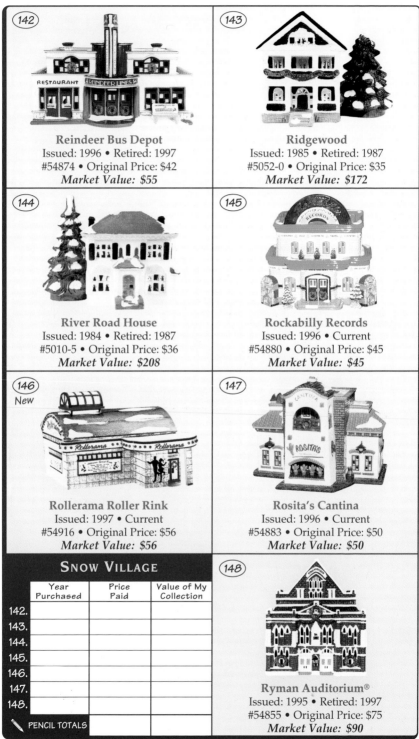

(142)

Reindeer Bus Depot
Issued: 1996 • Retired: 1997
#54874 • Original Price: $42
Market Value: $55

(143)

Ridgewood
Issued: 1985 • Retired: 1987
#5052-0 • Original Price: $35
Market Value: $172

(144)

River Road House
Issued: 1984 • Retired: 1987
#5010-5 • Original Price: $36
Market Value: $208

(145)

Rockabilly Records
Issued: 1996 • Current
#54880 • Original Price: $45
Market Value: $45

(146)
New

Rollerama Roller Rink
Issued: 1997 • Current
#54916 • Original Price: $56
Market Value: $56

(147)

Rosita's Cantina
Issued: 1996 • Current
#54883 • Original Price: $50
Market Value: $50

SNOW VILLAGE

	Year Purchased	Price Paid	Value of My Collection
142.			
143.			
144.			
145.			
146.			
147.			
148.			
PENCIL TOTALS			

(148)

Ryman Auditorium®
Issued: 1995 • Retired: 1997
#54855 • Original Price: $75
Market Value: $90

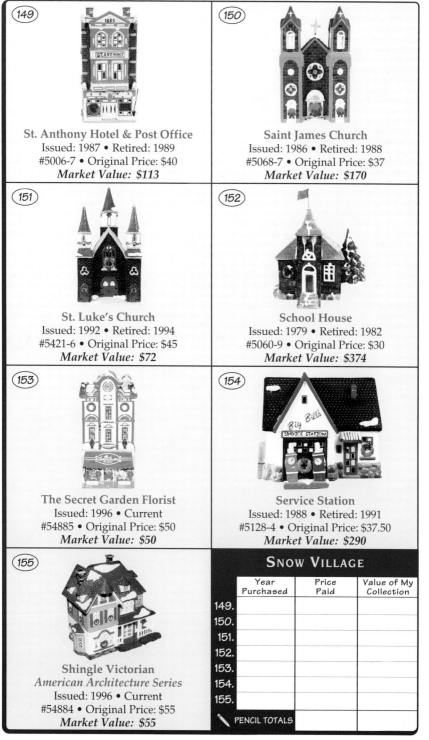

(149)

St. Anthony Hotel & Post Office
Issued: 1987 • Retired: 1989
#5006-7 • Original Price: $40
Market Value: $113

(150)

Saint James Church
Issued: 1986 • Retired: 1988
#5068-7 • Original Price: $37
Market Value: $170

(151)

St. Luke's Church
Issued: 1992 • Retired: 1994
#5421-6 • Original Price: $45
Market Value: $72

(152)

School House
Issued: 1979 • Retired: 1982
#5060-9 • Original Price: $30
Market Value: $374

(153)

The Secret Garden Florist
Issued: 1996 • Current
#54885 • Original Price: $50
Market Value: $50

(154)

Service Station
Issued: 1988 • Retired: 1991
#5128-4 • Original Price: $37.50
Market Value: $290

(155)

Shingle Victorian
American Architecture Series
Issued: 1996 • Current
#54884 • Original Price: $55
Market Value: $55

SNOW VILLAGE

	Year Purchased	Price Paid	Value of My Collection
149.			
150.			
151.			
152.			
153.			
154.			
155.			
✎ PENCIL TOTALS			

SNOW VILLAGE BUILDINGS

(156)

Single Car Garage
Issued: 1988 • Retired: 1990
#5125-0 • Original Price: $22
Market Value: $60

(157)

Skate & Ski Shop
Issued: 1994 • Current
#5467-4 • Original Price: $50
Market Value: $50

(158)

Skating Pond
Issued: 1982 • Retired: 1984
#5017-2 • Original Price: $25
Market Value: $375

(159)

Skating Rink/Duck Pond Set
Issued: 1978 • Retired: 1979
#5015-3 • Original Price: $16
Market Value: $1,000

(160)

Small Chalet
Issued: 1976 • Retired: 1979
#5006-2 • Original Price: $15
Market Value: $460

(161) *Version 2*

Small Double Trees
Issued: 1978 • Retired: 1989
#5016-1 • Original Price: $13.50
Market Value: $185 (red birds – $58)

Snow Village

	Year Purchased	Price Paid	Value of My Collection
156.			
157.			
158.			
159.			
160.			
161.			
162.			
✎ PENCIL TOTALS			

(162)

Smokey Mountain Retreat
(with magic smoking element)
Issued: 1996 • Current
#54872 • Original Price: $65
Market Value: $65

(163)

Snow Carnival Ice Palace (set/2)
Issued: 1995 • Current
#54850 • Original Price: $95
Market Value: $95

(164)

Snow Village Factory
Issued: 1987 • Retired: 1989
#5013-0 • Original Price: $45
Market Value: $138

(165)

Snow Village Resort Lodge
Issued: 1987 • Retired: 1989
#5092-0 • Original Price: $55
Market Value: $153

(166)

Shady Oak Church

Sunday School Serenade

Snow Village Starter Set (set/6)
Issued: 1994 • Retired: 1996
#5462-3 • Original Price: $50
Market Value: $78

(167)

Snowy Hills Hospital
Issued: 1993 • Retired: 1996
#5448-8 • Original Price: $48
Market Value: $80

(168)

Sonoma House
Issued: 1986 • Retired: 1988
#5062-8 • Original Price: $33
Market Value: $146

(169)

Southern Colonial
American Architecture Series
Issued: 1991 • Retired: 1994
#5403-8 • Original Price: $50
Market Value: $80

SNOW VILLAGE

	Year Purchased	Price Paid	Value of My Collection
163.			
164.			
165.			
166.			
167.			
168.			
169.			
PENCIL TOTALS			

SNOW VILLAGE BUILDINGS

(170)

Spanish Mission Church
Issued: 1990 • Retired: 1992
#5155-1 • Original Price: $42
Market Value: $80

(171)

Springfield House
Issued: 1987 • Retired: 1990
#5027-0 • Original Price: $40
Market Value: $82

(172)

Spruce Place
Issued: 1985 • Retired: 1987
#5049-0 • Original Price: $33
Market Value: $275

(173)

Starbucks® Coffee
Issued: 1995 • Current
#54859 • Original Price: $48
Market Value: $48

(174)

Steepled Church
Issued: 1976 • Retired: 1979
#5005-4 • Original Price: $25
Market Value: $555

(175)

Stone Church
Issued: 1977 • Retired: 1979
#5009-6 • Original Price: $35
Market Value: $600

SNOW VILLAGE

	Year Purchased	Price Paid	Value of My Collection
170.			
171.			
172.			
173.			
174.			
175.			
✏ PENCIL TOTALS			

Value Guide – Snow Village Buildings

176

Stone Church
Issued: 1979 • Retired: 1980
#5059-1 • Original Price: $32
Market Value: $970

177

Stone Mill House
Issued: 1980 • Retired: 1982
#5068-2 • Original Price: $30
Market Value: $500

178

Stonehurst House
Issued: 1988 • Retired: 1994
#5140-3 • Original Price: $37.50
Market Value: $66

179

Stratford House
Issued: 1984 • Retired: 1986
#5007-5 • Original Price: $28
Market Value: $180

180

Street Car
Issued: 1982 • Retired: 1984
#5019-9 • Original Price: $16
Market Value: $380

181

Stucco Bungalow
Issued: 1985 • Retired: 1986
#5045-8 • Original Price: $30
Market Value: $375

182

Summit House
Issued: 1984 • Retired: 1985
#5036-9 • Original Price: $28
Market Value: $352

Snow Village

	Year Purchased	Price Paid	Value of My Collection
176.			
177.			
178.			
179.			
180.			
181.			
182.			
PENCIL TOTALS			

Snow Village Buildings

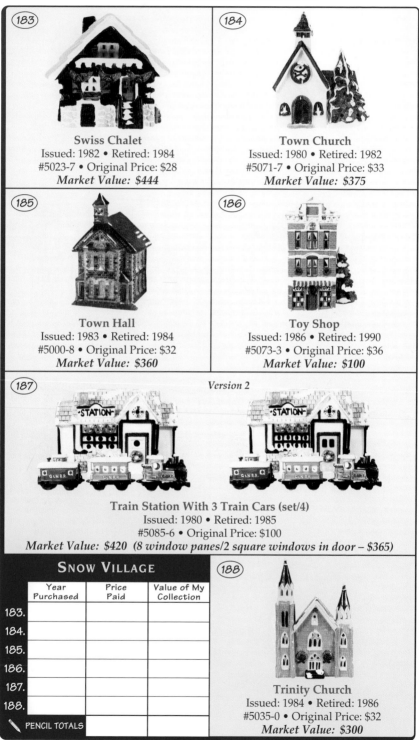

(183)

Swiss Chalet
Issued: 1982 • Retired: 1984
#5023-7 • Original Price: $28
Market Value: $444

(184)

Town Church
Issued: 1980 • Retired: 1982
#5071-7 • Original Price: $33
Market Value: $375

(185)

Town Hall
Issued: 1983 • Retired: 1984
#5000-8 • Original Price: $32
Market Value: $360

(186)

Toy Shop
Issued: 1986 • Retired: 1990
#5073-3 • Original Price: $36
Market Value: $100

(187)

Version 2

Train Station With 3 Train Cars (set/4)
Issued: 1980 • Retired: 1985
#5085-6 • Original Price: $100
Market Value: $420 (8 window panes/2 square windows in door – $365)

SNOW VILLAGE

	Year Purchased	Price Paid	Value of My Collection
183.			
184.			
185.			
186.			
187.			
188.			
✏ PENCIL TOTALS			

(188)

Trinity Church
Issued: 1984 • Retired: 1986
#5035-0 • Original Price: $32
Market Value: $300

(189)

Tudor House
Issued: 1979 • Retired: 1981
#5061-7 • Original Price: $25
Market Value: $302

(190)

Turn Of The Century
Issued: 1983 • Retired: 1986
#5004-0 • Original Price: $36
Market Value: $258

(191)

Twin Peaks
Issued: 1986 • Retired: 1986
#5042-3 • Original Price: $32
Market Value: $480

(192)

Victorian
Issued: 1979 • Retired: 1982
#5054-2 • Original Price: $30
Market Value: $340

(193)

Victorian Cottage
Issued: 1983 • Retired: 1984
#5002-4 • Original Price: $35
Market Value: $345

(194)

Victorian House
Issued: 1977 • Retired: 1979
#5007-0 • Original Price: $30
Market Value: $450

(195)

Village Church
Issued: 1983 • Retired: 1984
#5026-1 • Original Price: $30
Market Value: $415

SNOW VILLAGE

	Year Purchased	Price Paid	Value of My Collection
189.			
190.			
191.			
192.			
193.			
194.			
195.			
PENCIL TOTALS			

SNOW VILLAGE BUILDINGS

149

(196)

Village Greenhouse
Issued: 1991 • Retired: 1995
#5402-0 • Original Price: $35
Market Value: $65

(197)

Village Market
Issued: 1988 • Retired: 1991
#5044-0 • Original Price: $39
Market Value: $82

(198)

Village Police Station
Issued: 1995 • Current
#54853 • Original Price: $48
Market Value: $48

(199)

Village Post Office
Issued: 1992 • Retired: 1995
#5422-4 • Original Price: $35
Market Value: $75

(200)

Village Public Library
Issued: 1993 • Retired: 1997
#5443-7 • Original Price: $55
Market Value: $58

(201)

Village Realty
Issued: 1990 • Retired: 1993
#5154-3 • Original Price: $42
Market Value: $76

SNOW VILLAGE

	Year Purchased	Price Paid	Value of My Collection
196.			
197.			
198.			
199.			
200.			
201.			
202.			
PENCIL TOTALS			

(202)

Village Station
Issued: 1992 • Retired: 1997
#5438-0 • Original Price: $65
Market Value: $68

203

Village Station And Train (set/2)
Issued: 1988 • Retired: 1992
#5122-5 • Original Price: $65
Market Value: $115

204

Village Vet And Pet Shop
Issued: 1992 • Retired: 1995
#5427-5 • Original Price: $32
Market Value: $70

205

Village Warming House
Issued: 1989 • Retired: 1992
#5145-4 • Original Price: $42
Market Value: $72

206

Waverly Place
Issued: 1986 • Retired: 1986
#5041-5 • Original Price: $35
Market Value: $310

207

Wedding Chapel
Issued: 1994 • Current
#5464-0 • Original Price: $55
Market Value: $55

208

Williamsburg House
Issued: 1985 • Retired: 1988
#5046-6 • Original Price: $37
Market Value: $155

209

Woodbury House
Issued: 1993 • Retired: 1996
#5444-5 • Original Price: $45
Market Value: $64

SNOW VILLAGE BUILDINGS

SNOW VILLAGE

	Year Purchased	Price Paid	Value of My Collection
203.			
204.			
205.			
206.			
207.			
208.			
209.			
PENCIL TOTALS			

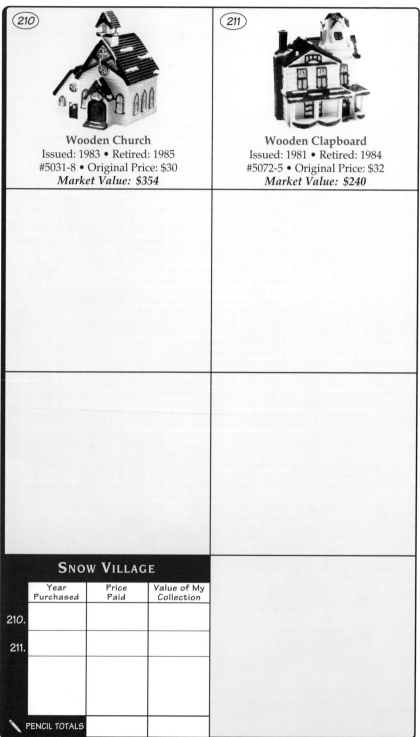

210

Wooden Church
Issued: 1983 • Retired: 1985
#5031-8 • Original Price: $30
Market Value: $354

211

Wooden Clapboard
Issued: 1981 • Retired: 1984
#5072-5 • Original Price: $32
Market Value: $240

SNOW VILLAGE

	Year Purchased	Price Paid	Value of My Collection
210.			
211.			
PENCIL TOTALS			

SNOW VILLAGE TRIVIA QUIZ

How much do you know about Snow Village? To find out take our quiz and then check your score on page 174!

1. The "Village Streetcar" has carried passengers to desired Snow Village destinations since 1994. For what American city did Frank Julian Sprague design the first electric trolley in 1883?

2. What were the first six buildings in The Original Snow Village?

3. The "Sno-Jet Snowmobile" blazed a trail onto the Village scene in 1990 as a means of winter transportation. In what country did Joseph-Armand Bombardier first patent the snowmobile in the 1930s?

4. What was the first pet to live in Snow Village?

5. Authentic fabric awnings first appeared on which Snow Village building?

6. What was the first Snow Village building produced without a tree attached to its side?

7. How much are the double-dip ice cream cones at the "56 Flavors Ice Cream Parlor?"

8. "The Honeymooner Motel" opened its doors for business in Snow Village in 1991. In what West Coast city did the first "motor hotel" for automobile travelers open in 1925?

9. "Paramount Theater" proclaims two holiday classics on its marquee. Which movie is "now showing," and which movie is "coming soon?"

10. What is the only building in The Original Snow Village with an actual street address in its title?

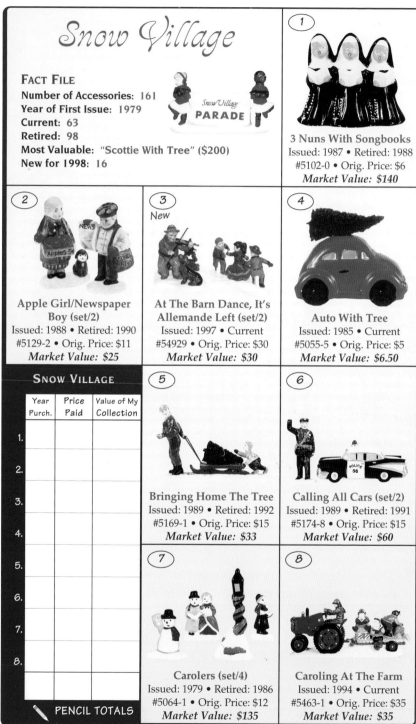

Snow Village

FACT FILE
Number of Accessories: 161
Year of First Issue: 1979
Current: 63
Retired: 98
Most Valuable: "Scottie With Tree" ($200)
New for 1998: 16

Snow Village
PARADE

1
3 Nuns With Songbooks
Issued: 1987 • Retired: 1988
#5102-0 • Orig. Price: $6
Market Value: $140

2
Apple Girl/Newspaper Boy (set/2)
Issued: 1988 • Retired: 1990
#5129-2 • Orig. Price: $11
Market Value: $25

3
New
At The Barn Dance, It's Allemande Left (set/2)
Issued: 1997 • Current
#54929 • Orig. Price: $30
Market Value: $30

4
Auto With Tree
Issued: 1985 • Current
#5055-5 • Orig. Price: $5
Market Value: $6.50

SNOW VILLAGE

	Year Purch.	Price Paid	Value of My Collection
1.			
2.			
3.			
4.			
5.			
6.			
7.			
8.			

✏ PENCIL TOTALS

5
Bringing Home The Tree
Issued: 1989 • Retired: 1992
#5169-1 • Orig. Price: $15
Market Value: $33

6
Calling All Cars (set/2)
Issued: 1989 • Retired: 1991
#5174-8 • Orig. Price: $15
Market Value: $60

7
Carolers (set/4)
Issued: 1979 • Retired: 1986
#5064-1 • Orig. Price: $12
Market Value: $135

8
Caroling At The Farm
Issued: 1994 • Current
#5463-1 • Orig. Price: $35
Market Value: $35

9

Caroling Family (set/3)
Issued: 1987 • Retired: 1990
#5105-5 • Orig. Price: $20
Market Value: $37

10

Caroling Through The Snow
Issued: 1996 • Current
#54896 • Orig. Price: $15
Market Value: $15

11

Ceramic Car
Issued: 1980 • Retired: 1986
#5069-0 • Orig. Price: $5
Market Value: $62

12

Ceramic Sleigh
Issued: 1981 • Retired: 1986
#5079-2 • Orig. Price: $5
Market Value: $65

13

Check It Out Bookmobile (set/3)
Issued: 1993 • Retired: 1995
#5451-8 • Orig. Price: $25
Market Value: $38

14

Children In Band
Issued: 1987 • Retired: 1989
#5104-7 • Orig. Price: $15
Market Value: $35

15

Choir Kids
Issued: 1989 • Retired: 1992
#5147-0 • Orig. Price: $15
Market Value: $33

16

Chopping Firewood (set/2)
Issued: 1995 • Current
#54863 • Orig. Price: $16.50
Market Value: $16.50

17

Christmas At The Farm (set/2)
Issued: 1993 • Retired: 1996
#5450-0 • Orig. Price: $16
Market Value: $26

18

Christmas Cadillac
Issued: 1991 • Retired: 1994
#5413-5 • Orig. Price: $9
Market Value: $20

SNOW VILLAGE

	Year Purch.	Price Paid	Value of My Collection
9.			
10.			
11.			
12.			
13.			
14.			
15.			
16.			
17.			
18.			

PENCIL TOTALS

SNOW VILLAGE ACCESSORIES

Value Guide – Snow Village Accessories

19

Christmas Children (set/4)
Issued: 1987 • Retired: 1990
#5107-1 • Orig. Price: $20
Market Value: $38

20
New

Christmas Kids (set/5)
Issued: 1997 • Current
#54922 • Orig. Price: $27.50
Market Value: $27.50

21

Christmas Puppies (set/2)
Issued: 1992 • Retired: 1996
#5432-1 • Orig. Price: $27.50
Market Value: $43

22

Christmas Trash Cans (set/2)
Issued: 1990 • Current
#5209-4 • Orig. Price: $6.50
Market Value: $7

23

Classic Cars (set/3)
Issued: 1993 • Current
#5457-7 • Orig. Price: $22.50
Market Value: $22.50

24

Coca-Cola® Brand Billboard
Issued: 1994 • Retired: 1997
#5481-0 • Orig. Price: $18
Market Value: $20

Snow Village

	Year Purch.	Price Paid	Value of My Collection
19.			
20.			
21.			
22.			
23.			
24.			
25.			
26.			
27.			
28.			

✏ **PENCIL TOTALS**

25

Coca-Cola® Brand Delivery Men (set/2)
Issued: 1994 • Current
#5480-1 • Orig. Price: $25
Market Value: $25

26

Coca-Cola® Brand Delivery Truck
Issued: 1994 • Current
#5479-8 • Orig. Price: $15
Market Value: $15

27

Cold Weather Sports (set/4)
Issued: 1991 • Retired: 1994
#5410-0 • Orig. Price: $27.50
Market Value: $50

28

Come Join The Parade
Issued: 1991 • Retired: 1992
#5411-9 • Orig. Price: $12.50
Market Value: $25

29

Country Harvest
Issued: 1991 • Retired: 1993
#5415-1 • Orig. Price: $13
Market Value: $30

30

Crack The Whip (set/3)
Issued: 1989 • Retired: 1996
#5171-3 • Orig. Price: $25
Market Value: $35

31

Doghouse/Cat In Garbage Can (set/2)
Issued: 1988 • Retired: 1992
#5131-4 • Orig. Price: $15
Market Value: $30

32

Down The Chimney He Goes
Issued: 1990 • Retired: 1993
#5158-6 • Orig. Price: $6.50
Market Value: $18

33

Early Morning Delivery (set/3)
Issued: 1992 • Retired: 1995
#5431-3 • Orig. Price: $27.50
Market Value: $40

34
New

Everybody Goes Skating At Rollerama (set/2)
Issued: 1997 • Current
#54928 • Orig. Price: $25
Market Value: $25

35

Family Mom/Kids, Goose/Girl (set/2)
Issued: 1985 • Retired: 1988
#5057-1 • Orig. Price: $11
Market Value: $45

36
New

Farm Accessory Set (set/35)
Issued: 1997 • Current
#54931 • Orig. Price: $75
Market Value: $75

SNOW VILLAGE

	Year Purch.	Price Paid	Value of My Collection
29.			
30.			
31.			
32.			
33.			
34.			
35.			
36.			

✏ PENCIL TOTALS

SNOW VILLAGE ACCESSORIES

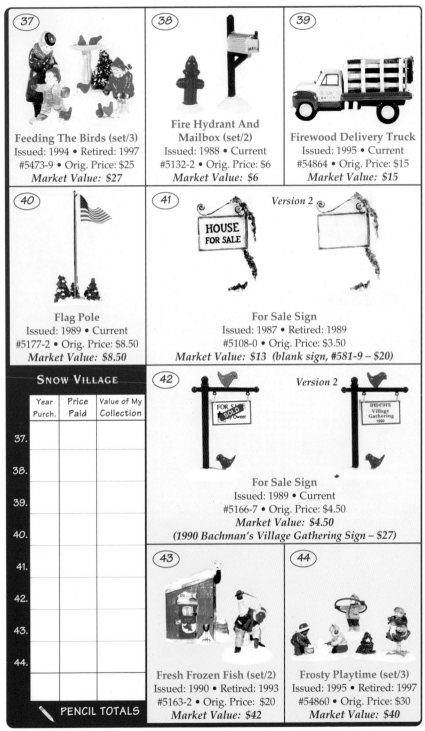

37

Feeding The Birds (set/3)
Issued: 1994 • Retired: 1997
#5473-9 • Orig. Price: $25
Market Value: $27

38

**Fire Hydrant And
Mailbox (set/2)**
Issued: 1988 • Current
#5132-2 • Orig. Price: $6
Market Value: $6

39

Firewood Delivery Truck
Issued: 1995 • Current
#54864 • Orig. Price: $15
Market Value: $15

40

Flag Pole
Issued: 1989 • Current
#5177-2 • Orig. Price: $8.50
Market Value: $8.50

41

Version 2

**HOUSE
FOR SALE**

For Sale Sign
Issued: 1987 • Retired: 1989
#5108-0 • Orig. Price: $3.50
Market Value: $13 (blank sign, #581-9 – $20)

42

Version 2

FOR SALE
SOLD
by Owner

BACHMAN'S
Village
Gathering
1990

For Sale Sign
Issued: 1989 • Current
#5166-7 • Orig. Price: $4.50
Market Value: $4.50
(1990 Bachman's Village Gathering Sign – $27)

43

Fresh Frozen Fish (set/2)
Issued: 1990 • Retired: 1993
#5163-2 • Orig. Price: $20
Market Value: $42

44

Frosty Playtime (set/3)
Issued: 1995 • Retired: 1997
#54860 • Orig. Price: $30
Market Value: $40

SNOW VILLAGE

	Year Purch.	Price Paid	Value of My Collection
37.			
38.			
39.			
40.			
41.			
42.			
43.			
44.			

✏ PENCIL TOTALS

45

**Girl/Snowman, Boy
(set/2)**
Issued: 1986 • Retired: 1987
#5095-4 • Orig. Price: $11
Market Value: $72

46

**Going To The
Chapel (set/2)**
Issued: 1994 • Current
#5476-3 • Orig. Price: $20
Market Value: $20

47

Grand Ole Opry Carolers
Issued: 1995 • Retired: 1997
#54867 • Orig. Price: $25
Market Value: $29

48

**Harley-Davidson®
Fat Boy & Softail**
Issued: 1996 • Current
#54900 • Orig. Price: $16.50
Market Value: $16.50

49

**A Harley-Davidson®
Holiday (set/2)**
Issued: 1996 • Current
#54898 • Orig. Price: $22.50
Market Value: $22.50

50

Harley-Davidson® Sign
Issued: 1996 • Current
#54901 • Orig. Price: $18
Market Value: $18

51

Hayride
Issued: 1988 • Retired: 1990
#5117-9 • Orig. Price: $30
Market Value: $70

52

New

**He Led Them Down The
Streets Of Town (set/3)**
Issued: 1997 • Current
#54927 • Orig. Price: $30
Market Value: $30

53

**Heading For The Hills
(2 assorted)**
Issued: 1996 • Current
#54897 • Orig. Price: $8.50
Market Value: $8.50

54

A Heavy Snowfall (set/2)
Issued: 1992 • Current
#5434-8 • Orig. Price: $16
Market Value: $16

SNOW VILLAGE

	Year Purch.	Price Paid	Value of My Collection
45.			
46.			
47.			
48.			
49.			
50.			
51.			
52.			
53.			
54.			

✏ PENCIL TOTALS

SNOW VILLAGE
ACCESSORIES

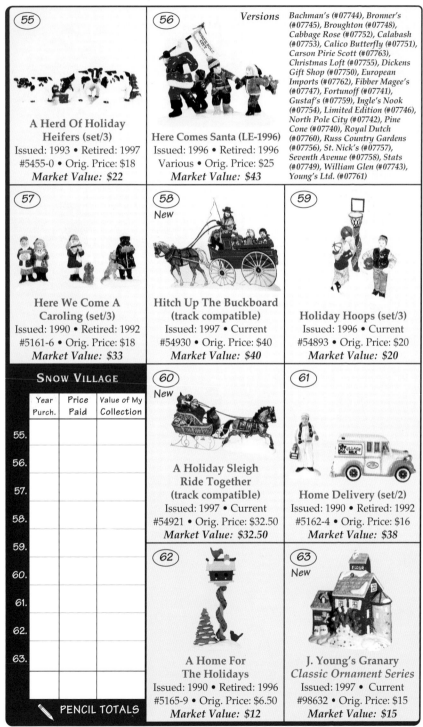

(55)

A Herd Of Holiday Heifers (set/3)
Issued: 1993 • Retired: 1997
#5455-0 • Orig. Price: $18
Market Value: $22

(56)

Versions

Here Comes Santa (LE-1996)
Issued: 1996 • Retired: 1996
Various • Orig. Price: $25
Market Value: $43

Bachman's (#07744), Bronner's (#07745), Broughton (#07748), Cabbage Rose (#07752), Calabash (#07753), Calico Butterfly (#07751), Carson Pirie Scott (#07763), Christmas Loft (#07755), Dickens Gift Shop (#07750), European Imports (#07762), Fibber Magee's (#07747), Fortunoff (#07741), Gustaf's (#07759), Ingle's Nook (#07754), Limited Edition (#07746), North Pole City (#07742), Pine Cone (#07740), Royal Dutch (#07760), Russ Country Gardens (#07756), St. Nick's (#07757), Seventh Avenue (#07758), Stats (#07749), William Glen (#07743), Young's Ltd. (#07761)

(57)

Here We Come A Caroling (set/3)
Issued: 1990 • Retired: 1992
#5161-6 • Orig. Price: $18
Market Value: $33

(58)

New

Hitch Up The Buckboard (track compatible)
Issued: 1997 • Current
#54930 • Orig. Price: $40
Market Value: $40

(59)

Holiday Hoops (set/3)
Issued: 1996 • Current
#54893 • Orig. Price: $20
Market Value: $20

SNOW VILLAGE

	Year Purch.	Price Paid	Value of My Collection
55.			
56.			
57.			
58.			
59.			
60.			
61.			
62.			
63.			
✎ PENCIL TOTALS			

(60)

New

A Holiday Sleigh Ride Together (track compatible)
Issued: 1997 • Current
#54921 • Orig. Price: $32.50
Market Value: $32.50

(61)

Home Delivery (set/2)
Issued: 1990 • Retired: 1992
#5162-4 • Orig. Price: $16
Market Value: $38

(62)

A Home For The Holidays
Issued: 1990 • Retired: 1996
#5165-9 • Orig. Price: $6.50
Market Value: $12

(63)

New

J. Young's Granary
Classic Ornament Series
Issued: 1997 • Current
#98632 • Orig. Price: $15
Market Value: $15

(64)

Just Married (set/2)
Issued: 1995 • Current
#54879 • Orig. Price: $25
Market Value: $25

(65) Version 2

approx. 5.5"   *approx. 4.5"*

Kids Around The Tree
Issued: 1986 • Retired: 1990
#5094-6 • Orig. Price: $15
Market Value: $64 (smaller – $45)

(66) New

Kids, Candy Canes . . . And Ronald McDonald® (set/3)
Issued: 1997 • Current
#54926 • Orig. Price: $30
Market Value: $30

(67)

Kids Decorating The Village Sign
Issued: 1990 • Retired: 1993
#5134-9 • Orig. Price: $12.50
Market Value: $27

(68) New

Kids Love Hershey's™! (set/2)
Issued: 1997 • Current
#54924 • Orig. Price: $30
Market Value: $30

(69)

Kids Tree House
Issued: 1989 • Retired: 1991
#5168-3 • Orig. Price: $25
Market Value: $60

(70) New

Let It Snow, Let It Snow (track compatible)
Issued: 1997 • Current
#54923 • Orig. Price: $20
Market Value: $20

(71)

U.S. MAIL

Mailbox
Issued: 1989 • Retired: 1990
#5179-9 • Orig. Price: $3.50
Market Value: $25

(72)

MAIL

Mailbox
Issued: 1990 • Current
#5198-5 • Orig. Price: $3.50
Market Value: $3.50

SNOW VILLAGE

	Year Purch.	Price Paid	Value of My Collection
64.			
65.			
66.			
67.			
68.			
69.			
70.			
71.			
72.			

✏ PENCIL TOTALS

SNOW VILLAGE ACCESSORIES

73

Man On Ladder Hanging Garland
Issued: 1988 • Retired: 1992
#5116-0 • Orig. Price: $7.50
Market Value: $22

74

Marshmallow Roast (set/3)
Issued: 1994 • Current
#5478-0 • Orig. Price: $32.50
Market Value: $32.50

75
New

McDonald's® ... Lights Up The Night
Issued: 1997 • Current
#54925 • Orig. Price: $30
Market Value: $30

76

Men At Work (set/5)
Issued: 1996 • Current
#54894 • Orig. Price: $27.50
Market Value: $27.50

77

Monks-A-Caroling
Issued: 1983 • Retired: 1984
#6459-9 • Orig. Price: $6
Market Value: $67

78

Monks-A-Caroling
Issued: 1984 • Retired: 1988
#5040-7 • Orig. Price: $6
Market Value: $50

SNOW VILLAGE

	Year Purch.	Price Paid	Value of My Collection
73.			
74.			
75.			
76.			
77.			
78.			
79.			
80.			
81.			
82.			

✏ PENCIL TOTALS

79

Moving Day (set/3)
Issued: 1996 • Current
#54892 • Orig. Price: $32.50
Market Value: $32.50

80

Mush! (set/2)
Issued: 1994 • Retired: 1997
#5474-7 • Orig. Price: $20
Market Value: $23

81

Nanny And The Preschoolers (set/2)
Issued: 1992 • Retired: 1994
#5430-5 • Orig. Price: $27.50
Market Value: $35

82
New

Nantucket
Classic Ornament Series
Issued: 1997 • Current
#98630 • Orig. Price: $15
Market Value: $15

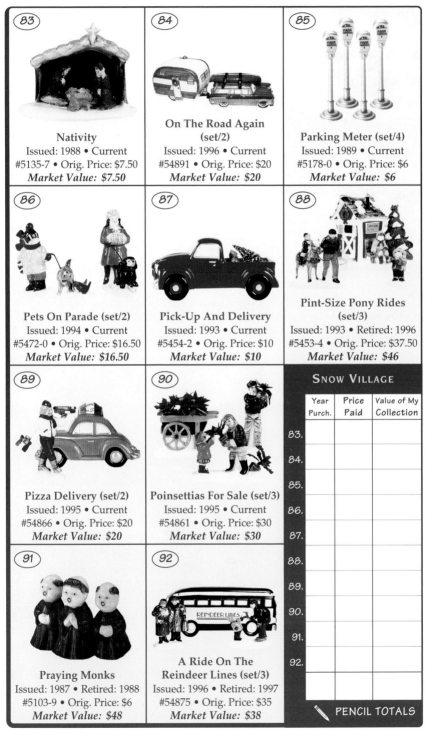

83

Nativity
Issued: 1988 • Current
#5135-7 • Orig. Price: $7.50
Market Value: $7.50

84

On The Road Again
(set/2)
Issued: 1996 • Current
#54891 • Orig. Price: $20
Market Value: $20

85

Parking Meter (set/4)
Issued: 1989 • Current
#5178-0 • Orig. Price: $6
Market Value: $6

86

Pets On Parade (set/2)
Issued: 1994 • Current
#5472-0 • Orig. Price: $16.50
Market Value: $16.50

87

Pick-Up And Delivery
Issued: 1993 • Current
#5454-2 • Orig. Price: $10
Market Value: $10

88

Pint-Size Pony Rides
(set/3)
Issued: 1993 • Retired: 1996
#5453-4 • Orig. Price: $37.50
Market Value: $46

89

Pizza Delivery (set/2)
Issued: 1995 • Current
#54866 • Orig. Price: $20
Market Value: $20

90

Poinsettias For Sale (set/3)
Issued: 1995 • Current
#54861 • Orig. Price: $30
Market Value: $30

91

Praying Monks
Issued: 1987 • Retired: 1988
#5103-9 • Orig. Price: $6
Market Value: $48

92

A Ride On The
Reindeer Lines (set/3)
Issued: 1996 • Retired: 1997
#54875 • Orig. Price: $35
Market Value: $38

SNOW VILLAGE

	Year Purch.	Price Paid	Value of My Collection
83.			
84.			
85.			
86.			
87.			
88.			
89.			
90.			
91.			
92.			

✏ PENCIL TOTALS

SNOW VILLAGE ACCESSORIES

93

Round And Round We Go! (set/2)
Issued: 1992 • Retired: 1995
#5433-0 • Orig. Price: $18
Market Value: $30

94

Safety Patrol (set/4)
Issued: 1993 • Retired: 1997
#5449-6 • Orig. Price: $27.50
Market Value: $30

95

Santa Comes To Town, 1995 (LE-1995)
Issued: 1994 • Retired: 1995
#5477-1 • Orig. Price: $30
Market Value: $45

96

Santa Comes To Town, 1996 (LE-1996)
Issued: 1995 • Retired: 1996
#54862 • Orig. Price: $32.50
Market Value: $40

97

Santa Comes To Town, 1997 (LE-1997)
Issued: 1996 • Retired: 1997
#54899 • Orig. Price: $35
Market Value: $38

98
New

Santa Comes To Town, 1998 (LE-1998)
Issued: 1997 • Current
#54920 • Orig. Price: $30
Market Value: $30

Snow Village

	Year Purch.	Price Paid	Value of My Collection
93.			
94.			
95.			
96.			
97.			
98.			
99.			
100.			
101.			
102.			

PENCIL TOTALS

99

Santa/Mailbox (set/2)
Issued: 1985 • Retired: 1988
#5059-8 • Orig. Price: $11
Market Value: $55

100

School Bus, Snow Plow (set/2)
Issued: 1988 • Retired: 1991
#5137-3 • Orig. Price: $16
Market Value: $60

101

School Children (set/3)
Issued: 1988 • Retired: 1990
#5118-7 • Orig. Price: $15
Market Value: $34

102

Scottie With Tree
Issued: 1984 • Retired: 1985
#5038-5 • Orig. Price: $3
Market Value: $200

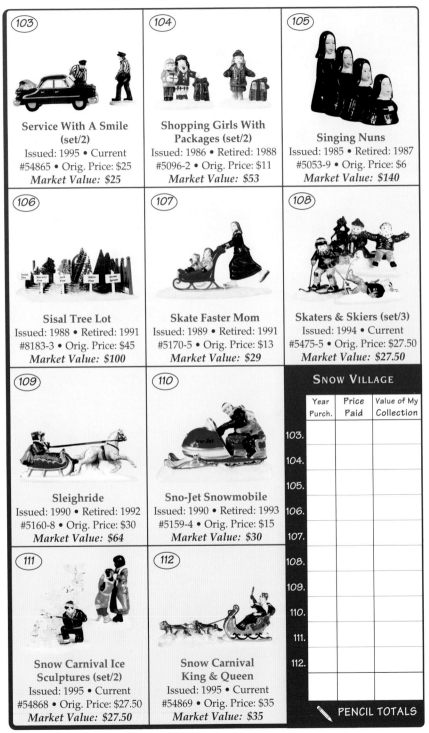

103

Service With A Smile (set/2)
Issued: 1995 • Current
#54865 • Orig. Price: $25
Market Value: $25

104

Shopping Girls With Packages (set/2)
Issued: 1986 • Retired: 1988
#5096-2 • Orig. Price: $11
Market Value: $53

105

Singing Nuns
Issued: 1985 • Retired: 1987
#5053-9 • Orig. Price: $6
Market Value: $140

106

Sisal Tree Lot
Issued: 1988 • Retired: 1991
#8183-3 • Orig. Price: $45
Market Value: $100

107

Skate Faster Mom
Issued: 1989 • Retired: 1991
#5170-5 • Orig. Price: $13
Market Value: $29

108

Skaters & Skiers (set/3)
Issued: 1994 • Current
#5475-5 • Orig. Price: $27.50
Market Value: $27.50

109

Sleighride
Issued: 1990 • Retired: 1992
#5160-8 • Orig. Price: $30
Market Value: $64

110

Sno-Jet Snowmobile
Issued: 1990 • Retired: 1993
#5159-4 • Orig. Price: $15
Market Value: $30

111

Snow Carnival Ice Sculptures (set/2)
Issued: 1995 • Current
#54868 • Orig. Price: $27.50
Market Value: $27.50

112

Snow Carnival King & Queen
Issued: 1995 • Current
#54869 • Orig. Price: $35
Market Value: $35

SNOW VILLAGE

	Year Purch.	Price Paid	Value of My Collection
103.			
104.			
105.			
106.			
107.			
108.			
109.			
110.			
111.			
112.			

✎ PENCIL TOTALS

SNOW VILLAGE ACCESSORIES

113

Snow Kids (set/4)
Issued: 1987 • Retired: 1990
#5113-6 • Orig. Price: $20
Market Value: $55

114

**Snow Kids Sled, Skis
(set/2)**
Issued: 1985 • Retired: 1987
#5056-3 • Orig. Price: $11
Market Value: $56

115

**Snow Village
Promotional Sign**
Issued: 1989 • Retired: 1990
#9948-1 • Orig. Price: N/C
Market Value: $24

116

Snowball Fort (set/3)
Issued: 1991 • Retired: 1993
#5414-3 • Orig. Price: $27.50
Market Value: $45

117

Snowman With Broom
Issued: 1982 • Retired: 1990
#5018-0 • Orig. Price: $3
Market Value: $14

118

Special Delivery (set/2)
Issued: 1989 • Retired: 1990
#5148-9 • Orig. Price: $16
Market Value: $52

SNOW VILLAGE

	Year Purch.	Price Paid	Value of My Collection
113.			
114.			
115.			
116.			
117.			
118.			
119.			
120.			
121.			
122.			
PENCIL TOTALS			

119

Special Delivery (set/2)
Issued: 1990 • Retired: 1992
#5197-7 • Orig. Price: $16
Market Value: $35

120

**Spirit Of Snow
Village Airplane**
Issued: 1992 • Retired: 1996
#5440-2 • Orig. Price: $32.50
Market Value: $43

121

**Spirit Of Snow
Village Airplane**
Issued: 1993 • Retired: 1996
#5458-5 • Orig. Price: $12.50
Market Value: $25

122

**Spirit Of Snow
Village Airplane**
Issued: 1993 • Retired: 1996
#5458-5 • Orig. Price: $12.50
Market Value: $25

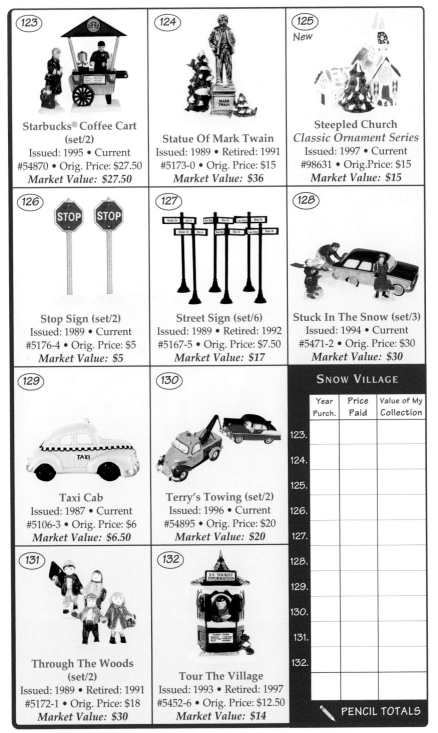

123

**Starbucks® Coffee Cart
(set/2)**
Issued: 1995 • Current
#54870 • Orig. Price: $27.50
Market Value: $27.50

124

Statue Of Mark Twain
Issued: 1989 • Retired: 1991
#5173-0 • Orig. Price: $15
Market Value: $36

125

New

Steepled Church
Classic Ornament Series
Issued: 1997 • Current
#98631 • Orig.Price: $15
Market Value: $15

126

Stop Sign (set/2)
Issued: 1989 • Current
#5176-4 • Orig. Price: $5
Market Value: $5

127

Street Sign (set/6)
Issued: 1989 • Retired: 1992
#5167-5 • Orig. Price: $7.50
Market Value: $17

128

Stuck In The Snow (set/3)
Issued: 1994 • Current
#5471-2 • Orig. Price: $30
Market Value: $30

129

Taxi Cab
Issued: 1987 • Current
#5106-3 • Orig. Price: $6
Market Value: $6.50

130

Terry's Towing (set/2)
Issued: 1996 • Current
#54895 • Orig. Price: $20
Market Value: $20

131

**Through The Woods
(set/2)**
Issued: 1989 • Retired: 1991
#5172-1 • Orig. Price: $18
Market Value: $30

132

Tour The Village
Issued: 1993 • Retired: 1997
#5452-6 • Orig. Price: $12.50
Market Value: $14

SNOW VILLAGE

	Year Purch.	Price Paid	Value of My Collection
123.			
124.			
125.			
126.			
127.			
128.			
129.			
130.			
131.			
132.			

✏ **PENCIL TOTALS**

SNOW VILLAGE ACCESSORIES

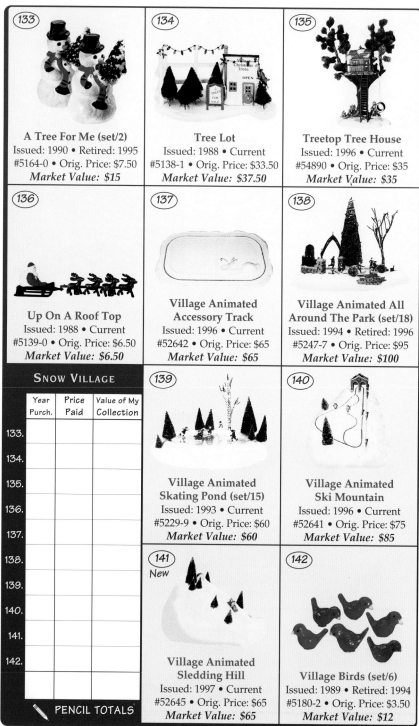

(133)

A Tree For Me (set/2)
Issued: 1990 • Retired: 1995
#5164-0 • Orig. Price: $7.50
Market Value: $15

(134)

Tree Lot
Issued: 1988 • Current
#5138-1 • Orig. Price: $33.50
Market Value: $37.50

(135)

Treetop Tree House
Issued: 1996 • Current
#54890 • Orig. Price: $35
Market Value: $35

(136)

Up On A Roof Top
Issued: 1988 • Current
#5139-0 • Orig. Price: $6.50
Market Value: $6.50

(137)

**Village Animated
Accessory Track**
Issued: 1996 • Current
#52642 • Orig. Price: $65
Market Value: $65

(138)

**Village Animated All
Around The Park (set/18)**
Issued: 1994 • Retired: 1996
#5247-7 • Orig. Price: $95
Market Value: $100

SNOW VILLAGE

	Year Purch.	Price Paid	Value of My Collection
133.			
134.			
135.			
136.			
137.			
138.			
139.			
140.			
141.			
142.			
PENCIL TOTALS			

(139)

**Village Animated
Skating Pond (set/15)**
Issued: 1993 • Current
#5229-9 • Orig. Price: $60
Market Value: $60

(140)

**Village Animated
Ski Mountain**
Issued: 1996 • Current
#52641 • Orig. Price: $75
Market Value: $85

(141)
New

**Village Animated
Sledding Hill**
Issued: 1997 • Current
#52645 • Orig. Price: $65
Market Value: $65

(142)

Village Birds (set/6)
Issued: 1989 • Retired: 1994
#5180-2 • Orig. Price: $3.50
Market Value: $12

143

Village Gazebo
Issued: 1989 • Retired: 1995
#5146-2 • Orig. Price: $27
Market Value: $45

144

Village Greetings (set/3)
Issued: 1991 • Retired: 1994
#5418-6 • Orig. Price: $5
Market Value: $12

145

Village Marching Band (set/3)
Issued: 1991 • Retired: 1992
#5412-7 • Orig. Price: $30
Market Value: $60

146

Village News Delivery (set/2)
Issued: 1993 • Retired: 1996
#5459-3 • Orig. Price: $15
Market Value: $25

147

Village Phone Booth
Issued: 1992 • Current
#5429-1 • Orig. Price: $7.50
Market Value: $7.50

148

Village Potted Topiary Pair
Issued: 1989 • Retired: 1994
#5192-6 • Orig. Price: $5
Market Value: $13

149

Village Streetcar (set/10)
Issued: 1994 • Current
#5240-0 • Orig. Price: $65
Market Value: $65

150

Village Up, Up & Away, Animated Sleigh
Issued: 1995 • Current
#52593 • Orig. Price: $40
Market Value: $40

151

Village Used Car Lot (set/5)
Issued: 1992 • Retired: 1997
#5428-3 • Orig. Price: $45
Market Value: $50

152

Village Waterfall
Issued: 1996 • Current
#52644 • Orig. Price: $65
Market Value: $65

SNOW VILLAGE

	Year Purch.	Price Paid	Value of My Collection
143.			
144.			
145.			
146.			
147.			
148.			
149.			
150.			
151.			
152.			
	PENCIL TOTALS		

SNOW VILLAGE ACCESSORIES

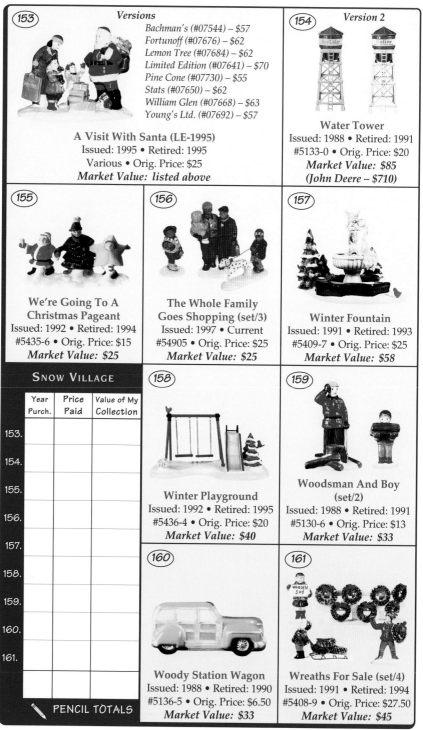

153

Versions

Bachman's (#07544) – $57
Fortunoff (#07676) – $62
Lemon Tree (#07684) – $62
Limited Edition (#07641) – $70
Pine Cone (#07730) – $55
Stats (#07650) – $62
William Glen (#07668) – $63
Young's Ltd. (#07692) – $57

A Visit With Santa (LE-1995)
Issued: 1995 • Retired: 1995
Various • Orig. Price: $25
Market Value: listed above

154

Version 2

Water Tower
Issued: 1988 • Retired: 1991
#5133-0 • Orig. Price: $20
Market Value: $85
(John Deere – $710)

155

We're Going To A Christmas Pageant
Issued: 1992 • Retired: 1994
#5435-6 • Orig. Price: $15
Market Value: $25

156

The Whole Family Goes Shopping (set/3)
Issued: 1997 • Current
#54905 • Orig. Price: $25
Market Value: $25

157

Winter Fountain
Issued: 1991 • Retired: 1993
#5409-7 • Orig. Price: $25
Market Value: $58

SNOW VILLAGE

	Year Purch.	Price Paid	Value of My Collection
153.			
154.			
155.			
156.			
157.			
158.			
159.			
160.			
161.			
✏ PENCIL TOTALS			

158

Winter Playground
Issued: 1992 • Retired: 1995
#5436-4 • Orig. Price: $20
Market Value: $40

159

Woodsman And Boy (set/2)
Issued: 1988 • Retired: 1991
#5130-6 • Orig. Price: $13
Market Value: $33

160

Woody Station Wagon
Issued: 1988 • Retired: 1990
#5136-5 • Orig. Price: $6.50
Market Value: $33

161

Wreaths For Sale (set/4)
Issued: 1991 • Retired: 1994
#5408-9 • Orig. Price: $27.50
Market Value: $45

1 New
The Carnival Carousel
(animated, musical)
Issued: 1998 • Current
#54933 • Orig. Price: $150
Market Value: $150

2 New
Haunted Mansion
(animated)
Issued: 1998 • Current
#54935 • Orig. Price: $110
Market Value: $110

3 New
Rock Creek Mill
Issued: 1998 • Current
#54932 • Orig. Price: $64
Market Value: $64

4 New
Snowy Pines Inn
Decorate The Tree
Snowy Pines Inn (set/9, Event Piece)
Issued: 1998 • Current
#54934 • Orig. Price: $65
Market Value: $65

5 New
Carnival Tickets &
Cotton Candy
Issued: 1998 • Current
#54938 • Orig. Price: $30
Market Value: $30

6 New
First Round Of The Year
(set/3, track compatible)
Issued: 1998 • Current
#54936 • Orig. Price: $30
Market Value: $30

7 New
Trick-Or-Treat Kids
(set/3)
Issued: 1998 • Current
#54937 • Orig. Price: $33
Market Value: $33

8 New
Two For The Road
(track compatible)
Issued: 1998 • Current
#54939 • Orig. Price: $20
Market Value: $20

9 New
The House That ♥ Built™
1998 (Event Piece)
Issued: 1998 • Current
#2210 • Orig. Price: N/A
Market Value: N/E

	Year Purch.	Price Paid	Value of My Collection
SNOW VILLAGE BUILDINGS			
1.			
2.			
3.			
4.			
ACCESSORIES			
5.			
6.			
7.			
8.			
OTHER COLLECTIBLES			
9.			
		PENCIL TOTALS	

*Ask your local retailer or check our website (www.collectorspub.com) for information on a special
Department 56 lighted piece to be announced in late June.*

Other Department 56 Collectibles

FACT FILE

The following buildings and accessories were manufactured by Department 56 but are not a part of either Heritage or Snow Village. Included here are two series, *Meadowland* and *Bachman's Hometown Series*, as well as Canadian and other exclusive pieces.

① Countryside Church
Issued: 1979 • Retired: 1980
#5051-8 • Orig. Price: $25
Market Value: $720

② Thatched Cottage
Issued: 1979 • Retired: 1980
#5050-0 • Orig. Price: $30
Market Value: $700

③ Aspen Trees
Issued: 1979 • Retired: 1980
#5052-6 • Orig. Price: $16
Market Value: $400

④ Sheep (set/12)
Issued: 1979 • Retired: 1980
#5053-4 • Orig. Price: $12
Market Value: $300

MEADOWLAND

	Year Purch.	Price Paid	Value of My Collection
1.			
2.			
3.			
4.			

BACHMAN'S HOMETOWN SERIES

1.			
2.			
3.			

CANADIAN EXCLUSIVES

1.			

① Hometown Boarding House
Issued: 1987 • Retired: 1988
#670-0 • Orig. Price: $34
Market Value: $320

② Hometown Church
Issued: 1987 • Retired: 1988
#671-8 • Orig. Price: $40
Market Value: $350

③ Hometown Drugstore
Issued: 1988 • Retired: 1989
#672-6 • Orig. Price: $40
Market Value: $585

① New
Canadian Trading Co.
(Canadian Exclusive For *Dickens' Village*)
Issued: 1997 • Current
#58306 • Orig. Price: $65*
Market Value: $65
*U.S. dollars

PENCIL TOTALS

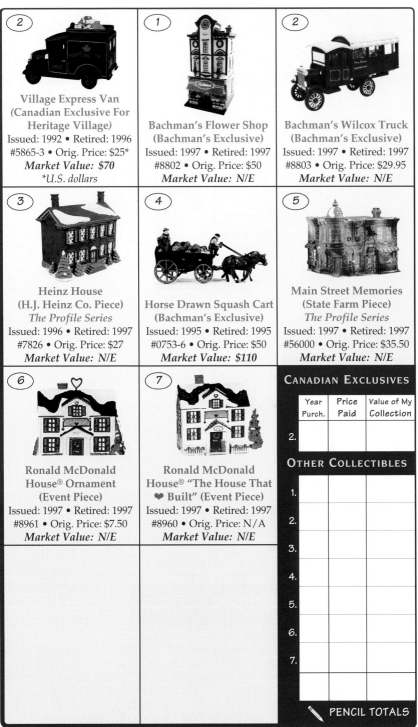

(2)

Village Express Van
(Canadian Exclusive For
Heritage Village)
Issued: 1992 • Retired: 1996
#5865-3 • Orig. Price: $25*
Market Value: $70
**U.S. dollars*

(1)

Bachman's Flower Shop
(Bachman's Exclusive)
Issued: 1997 • Retired: 1997
#8802 • Orig. Price: $50
Market Value: N/E

(2)

Bachman's Wilcox Truck
(Bachman's Exclusive)
Issued: 1997 • Retired: 1997
#8803 • Orig. Price: $29.95
Market Value: N/E

(3)

Heinz House
(H.J. Heinz Co. Piece)
The Profile Series
Issued: 1996 • Retired: 1997
#7826 • Orig. Price: $27
Market Value: N/E

(4)

Horse Drawn Squash Cart
(Bachman's Exclusive)
Issued: 1995 • Retired: 1995
#0753-6 • Orig. Price: $50
Market Value: $110

(5)

Main Street Memories
(State Farm Piece)
The Profile Series
Issued: 1997 • Retired: 1997
#56000 • Orig. Price: $35.50
Market Value: N/E

(6)

Ronald McDonald
House® Ornament
(Event Piece)
Issued: 1997 • Retired: 1997
#8961 • Orig. Price: $7.50
Market Value: N/E

(7)

Ronald McDonald
House® "The House That
♥ Built" (Event Piece)
Issued: 1997 • Retired: 1997
#8960 • Orig. Price: N/A
Market Value: N/E

Canadian Exclusives

	Year Purch.	Price Paid	Value of My Collection
2.			

Other Collectibles

1.			
2.			
3.			
4.			
5.			
6.			
7.			

✎ PENCIL TOTALS

OTHER COLLECTIBLES

TOTAL VALUE OF MY COLLECTION

Record the value of your collection here by adding the pencil totals from the bottom of each value guide page.

SNOW VILLAGE BUILDINGS

Page Number	Price Paid	Market Value
Page 121		
Page 122		
Page 123		
Page 124		
Page 125		
Page 126		
Page 127		
Page 128		
Page 129		
Page 130		
Page 131		
Page 132		
Page 133		
Page 134		
Page 135		
Page 136		
Page 137		
Page 138		
Page 139		
Page 140		
Page 141		
Page 142		
Page 143		
Page 144		
Page 145		
Page 146		
Page 147		
Page 148		
TOTAL		

SNOW VILLAGE BUILDINGS

Page Number	Price Paid	Market Value
Page 149		
Page 150		
Page 151		
Page 152		
Page 171		

SNOW VILLAGE ACCESSORIES

Page 154		
Page 155		
Page 156		
Page 157		
Page 158		
Page 159		
Page 160		
Page 161		
Page 162		
Page 163		
Page 164		
Page 165		
Page 166		
Page 167		
Page 168		
Page 169		
Page 170		
Page 171		

OTHER DEPARTMENT 56 COLLECTIBLES

Page 172		
Page 173		
TOTAL		

GRAND TOTALS

	PRICE PAID	MARKET VALUE

Snow Village Trivia Quiz Answers (from page 153)

1. Richmond, Virginia 2. "Country Church," "Gabled Cottage," "The Inn," "Mountain Lodge," "Small Chalet," "Steepled Church" 3. Canada 4. The black dog in "Scottie With Tree" (1984) who stayed for one year; he was retired in 1995 5. "The Secret Garden Florist" (1996) 6. "General Store" (1978), which had a small decorated tree on its porch roof 7. 5 cents 8. San Luis Obispo, California 9. "White Christmas" (now showing); "It's A Wonderful Life" (coming soon) 10. "2101 Maple"

*E*veryone's heard the stories: a friend of a friend is out for a Sunday drive, when they come upon a roadside tag sale. With little in mind other than spending a few minutes out in the warm sun, they decide to get out and take a look. Rummaging through the old records and dusty romance novels, something catches their eye. With a growing feeling of excitement they walk over to the end of the table and begin removing baby clothes from the top of a medium-sized white box. Their breath catches as they lift the white box and begin to gingerly remove nothing less than an authentic mint condition "Dickens' Village Mill." Holding their breath they walk up to the residents of the house and ask if this might possibly be for sale. Eagerly, they take out the ten dollars required to complete the sale . . . and run for their life.

If, however, your luck is not this good, you may be wondering how you can possibly acquire pieces for your villages that are not currently in production. To do this, you must turn to the secondary market, a term that may seem mystifying to those new to the world of collectibles. To better understand how the secondary market works, you must first understand how it came to be.

Retirements

In 1979, Department 56 made a decision that would change the world of "cottage collectibles" forever. With the Snow Village line having been in existence for three years, Department 56 began to realize that they could not keep coming out with exciting new releases and still maintain production of the existing product. So, in an effort to keep the line down to a manageable size, Department 56 announced that they would issue their first retirements.

Secondary Market Overview

These retirements secured the village's status as a collectible. Certain pieces were no longer available in stores and collectors who had perhaps missed a piece or were new to Department 56 found that they were unable to complete their collection by the usual means. In reverse of the economic principle, a demand was created. It was now time to find the supply.

The retired houses could only come from one source: the collector. Collectors started asking one another such questions as, "Just what would it take for you to part with that Snow Village 'Cathedral Church?'," and those with an eye on profit began to sell pieces of their collection. And so, before the ink on the retirement listings had finished drying, the Department 56 secondary market was born.

To this day, almost two decades later, the announcement of the retirements is an eagerly anticipated event, causing collectors to gather before the doors of their favorite Department 56 dealer on the appointed day each year. The retirement list is published in *USA Today* and, in keeping with the times, is also posted on the Internet that same morning on Department 56's own website, *www.department56.com*. Once the list is known to the public, the search begins for the elite retirements. Before you know it, the retail supplies are drained and, once again, collectors turn to the secondary market.

Retirements, however, are not the only reason for a piece to become coveted on the secondary market. Other factors (such as if a piece is limited either by time or production size, or if it was only produced for a special event, store or organization) can cause heavy interest on the secondary market and result in these pieces frequently commanding higher prices. However, it is important to remember that not all limited edition pieces are highly coveted; it all depends on the number of pieces produced, how much they cost and, of course, how popular they are with collectors.

Variations

Another aspect of the secondary market that may seem mind-boggling to the new collector is variations. Variations can occur for a multitude of reasons, human error and design modifications being the most common. Changes in structure or color can occur at any time during the life of a piece. These changes can come about as an attempt to facilitate production when problems arise, rectify overlooked errors (as was the case when the father from the "Amish Family" accessory briefly appeared on store shelves sporting a mustache), or to alter elements that the Department 56 designers feel "just aren't working."

Despite what you might think, Department 56 variations are not necessarily more limited than the regular version. There have been some errors that have been more prevalent on the market than the actual, "correct," piece. A perfect example of this is "Blythe Pond Mill House," which appeared with "By The Pond" inscribed as the title on the bottom of the cottage. It seems that more buildings were produced with the error than without. Therefore, if you are looking to purchase this piece on the secondary market, you should be looking for the building with the correct inscription, which has a higher secondary market value. When shopping the secondary market, however, always remember that not all variations will increase a building's market value.

Secondary Market Options

Now that you know a little bit about what the secondary market is, you may be wondering where you can find it. There are many ways in which collectors can buy and sell pieces on the secondary market. With time and patience you will be able to perfect a system that is not only comfortable for you, but capable of getting the results you desire, whether it's a quick sale or a large purchase of retired pieces.

When looking for a secondary market resource, one of the first places to get more information is to ask your local Department 56 retailer. Many retailers are adept at matching buyers with collectors that are looking to sell pieces from their villages. While most retailers are not directly involved in the secondary market, they may sponsor secondary market collector shows as a service to their customers. In any case, retailers are an invaluable source of secondary market information and are often a good place to begin your research into the secondary market in your region.

Perhaps the easiest and most direct way to reach other collectors is through a secondary market exchange service. Exchanges publish lists of pieces and asking prices on a monthly or, in a few instances, daily, basis and are a wonderful way to reach collectors all over the country. Exchange services act as middlemen in the transaction and a commission of 10-20% is usually the norm.

Collector's Club News

With the late 1997 introduction of an official collector's club for Department 56's Snowbabies figurines, many village collectors are holding their breath in anticipation of their very own club. Is it in the works? Only Department 56 knows the answer.

For now, many collectors enjoy independent local clubs where they can interact with other people who have caught the same "collecting bug." In fact, the idea of the "local chapter" has become so popular that over 100 independent clubs across the country have joined to form the National Council of "56" Clubs. You can contact them if you wish to start up a club in your own area. Write to:

National Council of "56" Clubs
651 *Perimeter Drive, Suite 600*
Lexington, KY 40517

There are some exchanges that sell only their own pieces, and in this case there would be no commission to complete the sale. There is usually a subscription or membership fee to receive an exchange's publication.

When looking for secondary market avenues it is always advisable to check out your local newsstand. Magazines written for collectors often feature their own "Swap & Sell" sections which work in much the same manner as exchange services. This may also be a good place to find exchange services or retailers active in the secondary market as they often take out advertisements in these sections. A few collectors place classified advertisements in their local newspaper (under Antiques/Collectibles), but it generally takes longer to sell pieces this way because newspapers reach a general readership and not collectors specifically.

As the Internet continues its growth explosion it is becoming the hottest place to buy and sell collectibles. Various sites publish on-line price listings, which are updated regularly. Also, the web is a wonderful source of information about Department 56 and collecting in general. By doing a search with keywords, such as "Department 56," "collectibles" or "secondary market," you are likely to be amazed at the number of sites and the magnitude of information you'll find. A word to the wise when dealing with the Internet, or for that matter, any resource: be wary of rumors.

Lastly, it's important to remember that not every building will soar in value, so if your sole reason to collect is for the investment, you may be disappointed. However, with common sense coupled with a taste for adventure, you will be assured of having not just a valuable and expansive collection, but also a network of friends with whom to share your collecting experience.

SECONDARY MARKET OVERVIEW

Exchanges, Dealers & Newsletters

Quarterly
(general information – *a must!*)
Department 56, Inc.
P.O. Box 44056
One Village Place
Eden Prairie, MN 55344-1056
(800) 548-8696

56 Directions
Jeff & Susan McDermott
364 Spring Street Ext.
Glastonbury, CT 06033
(860) 633-8192

Collectible Exchange, Inc.
6621 Columbiana Road
New Middletown, OH 44442
(800) 752-3208

The Cottage Locator
Frank & Florence Wilson
211 No. Bridebrook Rd.
East Lyme, CT 06333
(860) 739-0705

Dickens' Exchange
Lynda W. Blankenship
5150 Highway 22, Suite C-16
Mandeville, LA 70471
(504) 845-1954

*New England Collectibles
Exchange*
Bob Dorman
201 Pine Avenue
Clarksburg, MA 01247
(413) 663-3643

The Village Chronicle
Peter & Jeanne George
757 Park Ave.
Cranston, RI 02910
(401) 467-9343

The Village Press
Roger Bain
P.O. Box 556
Rockford, IL 61105-0556
(815) 965-0901

Villages Classified
Paul & Mirta Burns
P.O. Box 34166
Granada Hills, CA 91394-9166
(818) 368-6765

What The Dickens
Judith Isaacson
2885 West Ribera Place
Tucson, AZ 85742
(520) 297-7019

*W*hen insuring your collection, there are three major points to consider:

1 **Know your coverage** — Collectibles are typically included in homeowner's or renter's insurance policies. Ask your agent if your policy covers fire, theft, floods, hurricanes, earthquakes and damage or breakage from routine handling. Also, ask if your policy covers claims at "current replacement value" – the amount it would cost to replace items if they were damaged, lost or stolen – which is extremely important since the secondary market value of some pieces may well exceed their original retail price.

2 **Document your collection** — In the event of a loss, you will need a record of the contents and value of your collection. Ask your insurance agent what information is acceptable. Keep receipts and an inventory of your collection in a different location, such as a safe deposit box. Include the purchase date, price paid, size, issue year, edition limit/number, special markings and secondary market value for each piece. Photographs and video footage with close-up views of each piece are good back-ups.

> Many companies will accept a reputable secondary market price guide – such as the Collector's Value Guide™ – as a valid source for determining your collection's value.

3 **Weigh the risk** — To determine the coverage you need, calculate how much it would cost to replace your collection and compare it to the total amount your current policy would pay. To insure your collection for a specific dollar amount, ask your agent about adding a Personal Articles Floater or a Fine Arts Floater or "rider" to your policy, or insuring your collection under a totally separate policy. As with all insurance, you must weigh the risk of loss against the cost of additional coverage.

*W*ith Department 56's lighted houses and accessories the dream of building a perfect town can become a reality. What could be better than building a town without the hassles of planning and zoning committees, budget approval meetings (although in some households this may apply), building inspectors and the like? In building this town all you really need is patience, creativity and, most importantly, commitment.

Department 56 villages lend themselves to display like no other collectible. However, that display can be as simple or elaborate as you make it and there are many ways to make accent pieces like roads, mountains or ponds for your village. The best way to determine what works for you is to experiment, keeping in mind that there will always be some error in "trial and error."

To begin your display you must first choose a location. Take a look around your house and at your buildings. Try to estimate how much space you'll need, keeping in mind any special aspects of your buildings that you would like to highlight. If you are looking to set up one large display in a den or family room, you can use a table or set up a bench constructed of thick plywood and workhorses. A decorative tablecloth or sheet can be used to cover the edges and complement your design.

If one large display is not feasible because of space limitations, perhaps a series of smaller displays is more appropriate. Bookcases, bay windows and mantles are popular settings, while ladders, glass-front cabinets and staircases are also gaining in popularity. For a seasonal display, trim the branches of your Christmas tree and place your village beneath it, using a railroad set to enhance the perimeter of the village. Department 56 villages are also a beautiful addition to any holiday party when small vignettes are used as centerpieces.

To begin building your Department 56 display, it is a good idea to first design a blueprint of your village. Use a large sheet of paper and gently (use only pencil) trace the bottom of your buildings where you would like them to appear. Once you have penciled in the names of your buildings, stand back and visualize the scene that you want to achieve. Based on where the buildings are to be placed, sketch in all the large display items such as ponds, rivers and mountains that you want. Make sure that you maximize every bit of space as this will add realism to your village setting.

Some basic tools that you might like to have at your disposal before tackling a display project would include foam board, a hot glue gun, tacky wax, paint and props like plastic snow, rocks, moss and twigs. When you begin your display, it's best to start with the base and the lighting first, then set down the buildings and large display additions. Next come the trees, and finally the

accessories. Large display additions can be as simple or as complex as you like. Mountains, ponds, waterfalls and streams can be used to enhance any village and are a good way to add dimension to your display. These pieces can be purchased or can be made by hand. One of the benefits of using large display pieces is that they can be removed to provide space for new buildings as they are purchased. Therefore, you don't have to start from scratch with a new display every time you add a piece to your collection.

Once you have your large pieces where you wish, you can begin to add the personal touches. Department 56 has a large array of display accessories that you can purchase, including fences, lighted signs, trees and bridges (see *Current Display Pieces* section beginning on page 187). Also, with some creativity you can produce accessories for your village in your own home. In fact, anything is possible. For instance, you can make little planters by using painted jar tops and tiny dried flowers; a perfect addition to your park scene.

Finally, remember that there is no right way to display your collection. Pick themes that appeal to you and stir up feelings of nostalgia. After all, nothing warms the heart like happy memories.

Part of the fun of being a collector of Department 56 Villages is setting up your display. You may find that as you tentatively set up a couple of houses and shops in your village that your imagination may get the best of you. Great!

However, there are those who consider themselves "creatively challenged" and would prefer to follow a step-by-step guide. This section has something for everyone – shortcuts for those with a strong creative impulse, and clear-cut directions for those who would like to find out how the professionals do it.

We'll deal with two scenic elements: roads and ponds. Regardless of your scene, village or hills, you will need a base. Choose carefully from 1/2" or 1/4" plywood from your local lumber supply store. The 1/2" material is a bit more expensive, and somewhat heavier, but allows for easier movement. The 1/4" material is lighter, and quite fine for smaller, level displays of a village or town.

The Quick Road

You will need:

Masking tape
Small brush
Latex paint (black for modern city or suburban streets, brown
        for country or dirt roads, yellow and/or white for accents)
HO or N-scale model railroad ballast in gray and brown
        (check your local hobby shop)

Step One: Place your buildings on your display. Decide where you want your roads, and draw the rough contours on your base material. Remove the buildings and place masking tape along road outlines (ensures a clean line when painting). Paint the roads carefully into place. While the paint is wet, liberally sprinkle the ballast into the paint. Using small brush, lightly distribute the ballast to cover any wet areas. Let this dry 24 hours and gently vacuum the excess.

Step Two: Remove masking tape. Paint centerlines in road. Get fancy: Make stop lines, crosswalks and anything else you have ever seen on a street.

The Quick Pond

You will need:

Medium-sized brush
Small piece of plexiglass, or other clear, flat plastic
Several cans of spray paint (deep blue, light green & dark green)
Acrylic paint (optional)

Step One: Decide the approximate size of your pond, and spray one side only of the piece of plexiglass or

plastic with all three colors, randomly spraying each in sequence and leaving gaps between colors and between coats. If you spray small amounts of each, eventually your plexiglass will have mottled combinations of green/blue – like a pond or ocean. Let this dry.

Step Two: Place the painted side down into your scene and bring the edges of your grass, hills and mountains down over the edges of the plexiglass to give it the final shape you want. Add surrounding trees and bushes to your personal taste.

Step Three: With a medium-sized artist's brush, dab the acrylic medium over the top "unpainted" surface of your finished "water." It will look white going on, but will dry to simulate ripples and waves. Do not fear – try several small pieces until you get the results you like!

A great part of the appeal of collecting Department 56 is the creativity that the pieces inspire in creating displays. While there are many porcelain accessories offered within each collection in the line, Department 56 also offers a plethora of display accessories which can be used to complement the pieces in any of the villages. Some may be designed specifically for Heritage Village, Snow Village or *Dickens' Village* and are identified as (HV), (SV) or (DV), respectively. The new issues for 1998 are marked with an asterisk (*).

SNOW
- ❏ Blanket Of New
  Fallen Snow 49956
- ❏ Fresh Fallen Snow
  (7-oz. bag) 49979
- ❏ Fresh Fallen Snow
  (2-lb. box). 49980
- ❏ Real Plastic Snow
  (7-oz. bag) 49981
- ❏ Real Plastic Snow
  (2-lb. box). 49999

FENCES
- ❏ Candy Cane Fence 52664*
- ❏ Chain Link Fence
  (set/3) (SV) 52345
- ❏ Chain Link Fence
  Extensions (set/4) (SV). . 52353
- ❏ Courtyard Fence
  w/Steps (HV) 52205
- ❏ Snow Fence (SV) 52043
- ❏ Snow Fence, White (SV). 52657*
- ❏ Tree-Lined Courtyard
  Fence (HV). 52124
- ❏ Twig Snow Fence. 52598
- ❏ Victorian Wrought Iron
  Fence Extension (HV) . 52531
- ❏ Victorian Wrought Iron
  Fence and Gate
  (set/5) (HV) 52523
- ❏ White Picket Fence (SV). 51004
- ❏ White Picket Fence
  Extensions (set/6) (SV). 52625
- ❏ White Picket Fence
  w/Gate (set/5) (SV) . . . 52624
- ❏ Wrought Iron Fence
  (2 asst.) (HV) 59986

FENCES, CONT.
- ❏ Wrought Iron Fence
  (set/4) (HV) 59994
- ❏ Wrought Iron Fence
  Extension (set/9) (HV). 55158
- ❏ Wrought Iron Gate And
  Fence (set/9) (HV) 55140

TREES
- ❏ Arctic Pines (set/3). . . . 52608
- ❏ Autumn Trees (set/3) . . 52616
- ❏ Autumn Birch/Maple
  Tree (set/4) 52655*
- ❏ Bare Branch Trees
  (set/6) 52623
- ❏ Bare Branch Tree
  w/25 Lights. 52434
- ❏ Birch Tree Cluster 52631
- ❏ Cedar Pine Forest
  (set/3) 52606
- ❏ Double Pine Trees 52619
- ❏ Frosted Fir Tree
  (set/4) 52605
- ❏ Frosted Hemlock
  (set/2) 52638
- ❏ Frosted Norway
  Pines (set/3) 51756
- ❏ Frosted Spruce (set/2) . 52637
- ❏ Frosted Topiary (set/2). 52000
- ❏ Frosted Topiary (set/4). 52019
- ❏ Frosted Topiary
  (set/8, Asst. Lg.) 52027
- ❏ Frosted Topiary
  (set/8, Asst. Sm.) 52035
- ❏ Holly Tree 52630
- ❏ Jack Pines (set/3) 52622
- ❏ Pencil Pines (set/3). . . . 52469

Autumn Trees

Log Pile

CURRENT DISPLAY PIECES

*Snowy Scotch
Pines*

*Railroad
Crossing Sign*

*Mountain w/
Frosted Sisal
Trees, Sm.*

TREES, CONT.

❑ Pole Pine Forest
(set/5) 55271
❑ Pole Pine Tree, Lg. 55298
❑ Pole Pine Tree, Sm. . . . 55280
❑ Ponderosa Pines
(set/3) 52607
❑ Porcelain Pine
Trees (set/4) 59001*
❑ Snowy Evergreen
Trees, Lg. (set/5) 52614
❑ Snowy Evergreen
Trees, Med. (set/6) . . . 52613
❑ Snowy Evergreen
Trees, Sm. (set/6) 52612
❑ Snowy Scotch Pines
(set/3) 52615
❑ Towering Pines (set/2) . 52632
❑ Wagon Wheel
Pine Grove 52617
❑ Winter Birch (set/6) . . . 52636
❑ Wintergreen Pines
(set/2) 52661*
❑ Wintergreen Pines
(set/3) 52660*

MISCELLANEOUS ACCENT PIECES

❑ Acrylic Icicles (set/4) . . 52116
❑ Blue Skies Backdrop . . 52685*
❑ Boulevard Lampposts
(set/4) 52627
❑ Brick Road (set/2) 52108
❑ Brick Town Square . . . 52601
❑ Camden Park
Cobblestone Road (set/2). 52691*
❑ Camden Park Square
(set/21) (DV) 52687*
❑ Camden Park Square
Stone Wall (DV) 52689*
❑ Candy Cane Bench. . . . 52669*
❑ Christmas Eave Trim . . 55115
❑ City Subway
Entrance (HV) 55417
❑ Cobblestone Road (set/2). 59846
❑ Cobblestone Town
Square. 52602
❑ Country Road Lamp
Posts (set/4) 52663*
❑ Fallen Leaves
(3-oz. bag) 52610
❑ Flexible Sisal
Hedge (set/3) 52596
❑ Flexible Sisal Hedge,
Lg. (set/3). 52662*

MISCELLANEOUS ACCENT PIECES, CONT.

❑ Frosty Light Sprays
(set/2) 52682*
❑ Gazebo 52652*
❑ Hybrid Landscape
(set/22) 52600
❑ Landscape (set/14) 52590
❑ Let It Snow
Snowman Sign 52594
❑ Log Pile 52665*
❑ Magic Smoke
(6-oz. bottle). 52620
❑ Mill Creek Bridge 52635
❑ Mill Creek, Curved
Section 52634
❑ Mill Creek Park Bench . 52654*
❑ Mill Creek Pond. 52651*
❑ Mill Creek, Straight
Section 52633
❑ Mill Creek Wooden
Bridge 52653*
❑ Mountain Backdrop
(set/2) 5257-4
❑ Mountain Centerpiece . 52643
❑ Mountain Tunnel 52582
❑ Mountain w/
Frosted Sisal Trees,
Lg. (set/14). 5228-0
❑ Mountain w/
Frosted Sisal Trees,
Med. (set/8) 5227-2
❑ Mountain w/
Frosted Sisal Trees,
Sm. (set/5) 5226-4
❑ Mylar Skating
Pond (set/2) 5208-6
❑ Peppermint Road,
Curved Section 52667*
❑ Peppermint Road,
Straight Section 52666*
❑ Pine Point Pond 52618
❑ Pink Flamingos (set/4) . 52595
❑ Railroad Crossing
Sign (set/2) 55018
❑ Revolving Display
Stand. 52640
❑ Road Construction Sign
(set/2) (SV). 52680*
❑ Sisal Wreath (set/6) (SV). 54194
❑ Sled & Skis (set/2) 5233-7
❑ Starry Night
Sky Backdrop. 52686*
❑ Stone Curved
Wall/Bench (set/4) . . . 52650*

MISCELLANEOUS ACCENT PIECES, CONT.

- ❏ Stone Footbridge 52646*
- ❏ Stone Holly Corner
  Posts & Archway (set/3). 52648*
- ❏ Stone Holly Tree
  Corner Posts (set/2) . . . 52649*
- ❏ Stone Trestle Bridge. . . 52647*
- ❏ Stone Wall 52629*
- ❏ Tacky Wax 52175
- ❏ Telephone Poles
  (set/6) (SV). 52656*
- ❏ Television Antenna
  (set/4) (SV). 52658*
- ❏ Town Clock
  (2 asst.) 51101
- ❏ Two Lane Paved
  Road (SV). 52668*
- ❏ Village Square
  Clock Tower. 52591
- ❏ Walkway Lights (set/2). 52681*
- ❏ Weather Vane
  (set/5) (SV). 52659*
- ❏ Windmill (SV) 54569
- ❏ Wrought Iron
  Park Bench 52302

ELECTRICAL

- ❏ 6-Socket Light Set
  w/Bulbs 99279
- ❏ 20-Socket Light
  Set w/Bulbs 99278
- ❏ 45 LED Light Strand . . 52678*
- ❏ AC/DC Adapter 55026
- ❏ Double Light Socket
  Adapter. 99280*
- ❏ LED Light Bulb. 99247
- ❏ Lighted Christmas Pole,
  w/48 LED Lights. 52679*
- ❏ Lighted Christmas Tree
  w/50 LED Lights 52690*
- ❏ Lighted Snowy Tree
  w/Adapter 52683*
- ❏ Mini Lights. 52626
- ❏ Mini Lights
  (set/14 bulbs) 52159
- ❏ Multi Outlet Plug Strip. 99333
- ❏ Replacement
  Light Bulbs (set/3) 99244
- ❏ Replacement Round
  Light Bulbs (set/3) 99245
- ❏ Single Cord Set
  w/Switched Cord
  And Bulb 99028

ELECTRICAL, CONT.

- ❏ Spotlight (set/2). 52611
- ❏ Spotlight Replacement
  Bulbs (set/6) 99246
- ❏ String Of Starry Lights
  w/20 LED Lights 52684*
- ❏ Town Tree
  w/50 Lights. 52639
- ❏ Traffic Light (set/2) 55000
- ❏ Turn Of The Century . .
  Lamppost (set/4) 55042
- ❏ Utility Accessories
  (set/8: 2 stop signs,
  4 parking meters,
  2 traffic lights) (HV) . . 55123

LAMPS

- ❏ Double Street Lamps
  (set/4) 59960
- ❏ Street Lamps
  (set/6) (HV) 36366

VILLAGE BRITE LITES

- ❏ Adapter. 52256
- ❏ Angel 52671*
- ❏ Candles (set/4) 52674*
- ❏ Candy Canes (set/2) . . . 52670*
- ❏ Coca-Cola® Brand
  Neon Sign 54828
- ❏ Fence (set/4). 52361
- ❏ Holly Archway 52675*
- ❏ "Merry Christmas" 52230
- ❏ Reindeer 52248
- ❏ Santa 52396
- ❏ Santa In Chimney 52673*
- ❏ Snow Dragon 52672*
- ❏ Snowman 52370
- ❏ Tree 52388

*Village Square
Clock Tower*

*Stone Trestle
Bridge*

*Stone
Footbridge*

Merry Christmas

*Village Brite
Lites – "Merry
Christmas"*

SPOTLIGHT: THE HISTORICAL LANDMARK SERIES

*K*eeping with its strong sense of tradition, Department 56 introduced the *Historical Landmark Series* in 1997 as part of *Dickens' Village*. While conceptually based on the original English landmarks, these pieces reflect Department 56's interpretation of life in Dickens' times.

The first piece in the series, "Tower Of London," is a replica of the famous tower constructed by William of Normandy, who later became known as William the Conqueror. A cousin to England's King Edward, William was furious to discover that his cousin had revoked his promise to reward William his throne and instead passed it on to his brother-in-law, Harold. In response, William set out to conquer England. He completed this mission on October 14, 1066 when he met and defeated Harold at Hastings, becoming the next King of England. William then transformed the English countryside into a land of defense, ordering the building of fortresses throughout.

Construction of The Tower Of London began in 1078. By the time it was completed, it consisted of twenty towers and reached a height of over one hundred feet. Its strategic location overlooking London and the Thames River would provide England with a successful defensive tool throughout history. Then during his reign, King Henry III ordered the tower be whitewashed and renamed the White Tower, expanding the title "Tower Of London" to include the other towers as well. Since it's construction, the tower has served as the royal residence and a prison, as well as the site of the Public Records, the Royal Mint and the Crown Jewels.

SPOTLIGHT: THE HISTORICAL LANDMARK SERIES

The Department 56 "Tower Of London" focuses on the White Tower and rightfully so as this was the first to be constructed and stands proudly in the center of the 18 acre complex. The set includes a gate and tower as well as the Raven Master and six ravens. According to legend, the ravens symbolize England's strength and stability, which will remain as long as there are ravens living on the grounds. To this day, six ravens are maintained within the walls of The Tower Of London.

The second piece in the series, "The Old Globe Theatre" celebrates the spirit of the theater. Built circa 1599 in the London district of Bankside, the original theater burned to the ground in 1613. According to historians, the theater's demise was caused by the firing of a cannon during a performance of "Henry VIII" which sparked a fire on the gallery roof. It was rebuilt in 1614 on its original foundation, only to be torn down by Puritan reformists in 1642 in order to build tenements. It wasn't until more than three centuries later, in 1987, that reconstruction of the theater began again, about 200 yards from the original foundation.

A classic Elizabethan theater, the Globe served as a home for Lord Chamberlain's Men, a group of actors who performed Shakespeare's classics under the stars. While there are no confirmed pictures of the original theater, it is believed that the modern Globe more closely resembles the first than the second structure, as does the Department 56 rendition.

While each piece in the *Historical Landmark Series* offers a wealth of historical information, they are limited to one year of production, and are therefore sure to become a new annual tradition in the collecting of *Dickens' Village.*

GLOSSARY

accessory—pieces designed to enhance the display of Heritage and Snow Village buildings. Accessories are typically non-lit miniature figurines depicting people, vehicles, trees and more.

animated—a piece with motion. Department 56 has issued several animated pieces in recent years. New for 1998 is the "Village Animated Sledding Hill."

bottomstamp—also called an "understamp," these are identifying marks on the underside of a figurine or building. Buildings have a bottomstamp which includes the village name, the title of the piece, the copyright date and the Department 56 logo.

building—general term for miniature lighted shops, offices, homes, churches, etc.

catalog exclusives—Department 56 has offered early release of several "next year's introductions" to a group of retailers who participate in selected gift catalogs. During the introduction year, these pieces are usually available to Showcase Dealers as well.

collectibles—anything and everything that is "able to be collected," whether it's figurines, dolls . . . or even *whirligigs* can be considered a "collectible," but it is generally recognized that a true collectible should be something that increases in value over time.

Gift Creations Concepts (GCC)—a syndicated catalog group which includes over 300 retail stores.

Gold Key Dealers—Showcase retailers who are recognized for outstanding commitment to the Department 56 product line. This is the highest distinction a retailer can achieve.

history list—Department 56 brochures which list the item number, title, issue year, suggested retail price and retirement year of pieces.

International Collectible Exposition (I.C.E.)—national collectible shows held in Rosemont, Illinois each June or July and in April alternating between Edison, New Jersey (1998) and Long Beach, California (1999).

issue date—for Department 56, the year of production is considered the year of "issue," although the piece may not become available to collectors until the following year.

limited edition (LE)—a piece scheduled for a predetermined production quantity or time period. Some Heritage Village pieces have been limited to a specific number of pieces (ex. "Ramsford Palace" was limited to 17,500 pieces) or limited by year of production (ex. "The Old Globe Theater" is limited to 1998 production).

markings—any of the various identifying features found on a collectible. It can be information found on bottomstamps or backstamps, an artist's signature or even a symbol denoting a specific year or artist.

mid-year introductions—additional Department 56 pieces are announced in May, which is a follow-up to the major January introductions. These pieces are usually available in smaller allocations than January introductions during the first year, but become readily available in subsequent years.

mint condition—piece offered for sale on the secondary market in "like-new" condition. Mint-in-box means the piece is still in its original box.

open edition—a piece with no pre-determined limitation on time or size of production run.

porcelain—the hard and non-absorbent material used to make Department 56 buildings; a kind of ceramic made primarily with kaolin (a pure form of clay).

primary market—the conventional collectibles purchasing process in which collectors buy at issue price through retail stores, direct mail or home shopping networks.

real estate—colloquial term for the subsection of the collectibles industry that features small-scale buildings, cottages and villages.

release date—the year a piece becomes available to collectors. For most pieces, the release date is the year following the issue date.

retired—a piece which is taken out of production, never to be made again, usually followed by a scarcity of the piece and a rise in value on the secondary market.

secondary market—the source for buying and selling collectibles according to basic supply-and-demand principles ("pay what the market will bear"). Popular pieces, retired or with low production quantities can appreciate in value far above the original retail issue price.

series—a special grouping within a collection based on a certain theme, such as the *American Architecture Series* in Snow Village.

Showcase Dealers—a select group of retailers who receive early shipments of new and limited edition pieces. These retailers have a strong retail display supported with good inventory.

sleeve—thin cardboard packaging that slips over a Styrofoam™ box, usually illustrated with information such as the name of the collection, name of the piece and a black & white photograph of the piece.

track compatible—pieces that can stand alone, but are made to go with animated tracks, such as Snow Village's "Let It Snow, Let It Snow."

All Heritage and Snow Village pieces are listed below in alphabetical order. The first number refers to the piece's location within the Value Guide section and the second to the box in which it is pictured on that page. Items that are not pictured are listed as "NP."

ALPHABETICAL INDEX

– Key –

All Heritage and Snow Village pieces are listed below in numerical order by stock number. The first number refers to the piece's location within the Value Guide section and the second to the box in which it is pictured on that page. Items that are not pictured are listed as "NP."

Look for these other